TREES, LANDSCAPES AND YOU

To my man Mike!
You're a good man to know and a great inspiration. I hope you enjoy the book!
All the Best,
Paul M.

TREES, LANDSCAPES AND YOU

Paul Francis Martin
ISA-Certified Arborist (International Society of Arboriculture)
Growing Earth Tree Care

Copyright © 2015 Paul Francis Martin
All rights reserved.

ISBN: 1502791277
ISBN 13: 9781502791276

I dedicate Trees, Landscapes, and You *to Jesus and to my wonderful family: my lovely wife, Nalan, and my three fabulous children—Tarkan, Manolya, and Joshua. You guys inspire me in everything I do, and my world would be empty without you. I also dedicate this book to the hardworking arborists at Growing Earth Tree Care, especially my brother and business partner, Jim. I love you guys! Paul Francis Martin*

CONTENTS

	Preface	ix
Chapter 1	Designing Your Landscape	1
Chapter 2	Changing Landscapes	5
Chapter 3	Composting	8
Chapter 4	Green, Green, the Grass Is Green!	11
Chapter 5	Your Garden: Spring into Summer	14
Chapter 6	Garden Path Plantings	18
Chapter 7	Fall Perennials	22
Chapter 8	The Cooling Effect of Trees	24
Chapter 9	The Life Cycle of Trees	26
Chapter 10	The Amazing Leaf!	29
Chapter 11	Tree Selection and Planting Tips	32
Chapter 12	The Importance of Good Soil	35
Chapter 13	Mulch for Your Trees	36
Chapter 14	Fertilizing	39
Chapter 15	Plant Your Christmas Tree!	41
Chapter 16	Winter Tree Care	44
Chapter 17	Water Your Trees This Summer	47
Chapter 18	Eight Signs of Trouble with Your Trees	49
Chapter 19	Let's Get to the Root of the Problem	52
Chapter 20	Urban Tree Stress	56
Chapter 21	Tree Pests and Disease	62
Chapter 22	Hemlock Woolly Adelgid	66

Chapter 23	Borers and the Damage They Cause · · · · · · · · · · · · · · · · · 69
Chapter 24	Why Won't You Top My Trees? · · · · · · · · · · · · · · · · · · · 71
Chapter 25	What Makes Some Trees More Likely to Fail during a Storm? · 74
Chapter 26	Safety around Storm-Damaged Trees · · · · · · · · · · · · · · · 77
Chapter 27	Cabling Systems in Trees · 79
Chapter 28	Will Your Construction Project Kill Your Trees? · · · · · · 82
Chapter 29	Homeowner Associations and Their Trees · · · · · · · · · · · 86
Chapter 30	Is Your Tree Structurally Sound? · · · · · · · · · · · · · · · · · · · 90
Chapter 31	Consulting Arborists · 94
Chapter 32	Property-Line Disputes · 98
Chapter 33	How Much Is That Tree Worth? · · · · · · · · · · · · · · · · · · 101
	About the Author · 107

PREFACE

Trees, Landscapes, and You is a compilation of articles written by industry professionals. Many of the chapters contained within this book were written by Paul Francis Martin, ISA-certified arborist and owner of Growing Earth Tree Care in northern Virginia. Author background information is provided at the beginning of the first chapter written by authors other than Martin; their names and titles alone are listed in subsequent chapters.

The book covers a wide variety of tree and landscape topics of interest to property owners or anyone wishing to learn more about their surrounding landscape. It can be read cover to cover or simply used as a handy reference. The articles provide useful and practical information to guide you in understanding and making decisions for your yard—from pruning to designing layouts, from ridding plants of pesky bugs to assessing the health and strength of your trees.

The authors and publisher do not claim to offer legal or professional advice for your particular situation. Since every situation and circumstance is different, please consult with an industry expert prior to making or accepting any diagnosis or important decisions. This book is published for enjoyment and informational purposes only.

CHAPTER 1

DESIGNING YOUR LANDSCAPE

The formal garden above is located at the Oatlands Plantation in northern Virginia.

So you've decided it's time for a change. Perhaps you want to turn your plain yard into a beautifully landscaped wonder. How should you go about it? What features should you include? Should you hire a landscape architect or attempt to design it yourself? Should you engage a firm to install your newly designed landscape, or do you want to feel the dirt in your own hands and enjoy that sense of accomplishment? This chapter may help answer some of these questions and start you on your way.

As you work through the planning process, it's a good idea to establish a budget. If you're handy and can do most of the work yourself, you can stretch a small budget and get the most out of it. Conversely, if you're not so good with your hands, or you simply don't have the time, you will need to work with landscapers to do the installation. Either way, your budget will dictate how elaborate or simple your design should be. You may want to do the landscape installation in phases to accommodate your cash flow; your plans should reflect the various stages. If you decide to work with a landscape designer, which is certainly a good idea, you may be interested to know that some nurseries offer the services of their landscape designers at no charge.

Think of your property as a blank canvas and yourself as an artist. At the same time, think about how you would get the most enjoyment from your yard. Would you like to entertain on the back patio by hosting summer barbecues with family and friends? Or would you prefer quiet gardens with winding paths where you can meditate and take a mental vacation at the end of a hard day at the office? Or would you enjoy a little of both? Perhaps you want open areas for children to play or garden areas for growing produce. Your overall purpose will help guide your decisions as you choose which features to incorporate within the design.

Now assess your property's current site conditions. Are there any existing focal points, such as specimen trees, a gorgeous backdrop view, a pond, or other prominent features, that you can highlight? How can you incorporate the architecture of the house into your plan? What about the topography? How does water flow across the property? Does it drain well, or do you have wet areas? Can those wet areas be used as wetlands within your design, or will it be necessary to make changes to mitigate the problem?

Once you've thought about the landscape assets that you would like to focus on or at least keep intact, you can start to fill in the missing pieces of your new design. Start collecting ideas from magazines, other properties, the nursery, and the web. As you enhance the plan with patios, gazebos, gardens, winding pathways, walls, trellises, fountains, and other elements, keep in mind your overall use and enjoyment goals. Make sure each new item helps to achieve those goals. A good plan will also take into consideration such seasonal aspects as the timing of blossoms and fall color. If privacy is a concern, border trees or fencing are important factors that you don't want to leave out.

Consider the flow of water across your property as you plan the design. Changes in the flow can adversely affect the health of trees by either flooding or restricting water to their root zones. It could also affect your neighbor's landscape as well. This is especially important when you are planning to change the site by grading or with the installation of retaining walls and other hardscape items.

Do you like water features such as birdbaths, fountains, waterfalls, or ponds? These items can be small additions or large focal points, depending upon their size and placement within the landscape. You want to avoid standing water, because it can attract mosquitos and other problems; circulation and movement are critical.

As your plan comes together, you can concentrate on some of the details. Consider a well-placed bench along a pathway or beside a pond or perhaps a wooden walking bridge over a wet area. Something as simple as a large stone in the middle of a garden or wild grass along a border area can have a big impact. If your space is limited, you may want to consider potted and hanging plants. You can always combine form with function by planting a vegetable garden.

Keep in mind the mature size of plantings, especially trees. A common mistake, even for landscape designers, is overcrowding. You want to space trees and other plantings properly to avoid having to thin things out in a few short years. Simple designs often have a more pleasing visual impact than complicated, overcrowded ones, and they are easier to maintain.

In most cases, it's best to plant trees in groups rather than in isolation. They benefit from shared root zones and tend to protect each other from strong winds, droughts, and other natural calamities. Furthermore, a two- to three-inch layer of mulch over the entire root-zone area will help define it and provide nutrients for the soil.

When adding trees to the landscape, don't overplant any one species. Instead, plant a variety of native trees to enhance your landscape; that way, you will also minimize insect and disease problems. Be sure to plant the right tree in the right place. Keep in mind that each tree needs particular soil conditions, water flow, sunlight, and overall space for growth.

It's exciting to design and make changes to your landscape. With a little planning and some help from the experts at your local nursery, you can have that oasis you've always dreamed about.

CHAPTER 2
CHANGING LANDSCAPES

LANDSCAPES ARE CONSTANTLY GROWING, WHICH means they're constantly changing. Keeping up with the changes requires vigilance. Even the most well-planned landscape will need to be pruned and have deadwood removed, weeds taken out, and plant material replaced now and then.

A common problem we see with landscapes is overplanting or placing new plantings too close together. Landscapes designed to give instant results often do not take future growth into consideration. A correctly installed planting will allow enough room for the trees and other plantings to grow to maturity. But there's often a tug-of-war between having the landscape you want now and the one that will show up down the road. One solution to this dilemma is *planned obsolescence*: install some temporary plantings that you'll replace or thin out as time goes by and landscape conditions change.

It's important to keep an eye on sunlight and water flow as your landscape grows. Sunny areas may become shaded in a few years, which can have negative consequences for lower-level, sun-loving trees, bushes, and flowers. Pruning for sunlight may become necessary as trees and other tall plantings fill in. Water availability can be affected as an increasing canopy begins to restrict the amount of water reaching ground level and lower-profile plants. If an irrigation system is used, adjustments may become necessary.

Although a landscape designed with growth in mind will reduce the need for pruning and removals, even the best plans will not eliminate it. Pruning is an essential practice for keeping trees and bushes healthy. Deadwood and branches that are crossing and rubbing, diseased, dying, or weakly attached are obvious candidates for pruning, along with branches growing into or over other landscape features. Plant-growth regulators can limit the overall size of trees by restricting the growth between branch nodes and by reducing leaf size. This can cut down on the need for pruning and may offer some health benefits, including an increase in fibrous, absorbing roots and disease and drought resistance. However, plant-growth regulators may not be appropriate for all trees and situations. Check with your arborist to see if it might help with your landscape maintenance.

Weeds can be a constant source of frustration, but there are ways to limit their havoc. The best strategy is to be diligent. The more you neglect dealing with them, the more they will take over like an invading army. The best way to deal with weeds is to make their habitat less desirable. Healthy growing plants can often shade them out, and a two- to three-inch layer of mulch can keep them to a minimum. Weed killers are not recommended in most situations, because the root systems of nearby desirable plant materials can absorb the poison. The old-fashioned method of pulling them out by their roots may still be the best way to control weeds in your landscape. You might want to consider paying a bounty to the neighborhood kids. This will not only keep your weeds under control, but it will also help the neighborhood economy.

The growing and evolving landscape gives you opportunities to make changes as time goes on. Replacement plantings can bring new colors, smells, and shapes to liven things up. Think outside the box and try different species, but keep in mind that natives fare better in general. Remember that variety is not only the spice of life—it also makes for a more pest-resistant and visually pleasing landscape.

Plan for the future when you install your landscape. For instance, fast-growing trees along the property border can offer screening from the neighbor's property in the early years. But fast-growing trees tend to be short-lived and often develop structural problems as they outgrow themselves. A good plan might be to plant the fast-growing trees along the border and also plant more desirable, slower-growing species just inside the border. By the time the more desirable trees are established and start filling in, the faster growing trees can be selectively removed as you thin them out of the landscape. The results will be beneficial in both the short and long runs.

In addition, try to anticipate problems during the planning process. If you have water features such as a pool, pond, or fountain, avoid planting trees that will drop leaves or other debris into these sensitive areas. You also want to select species that will keep pathways and other areas clear from fast-growing, encroaching branches. This can be done by your choice of plant material or by moving its planting location farther away.

Professionals, such as landscape architects, certified arborists, and even the experts at your local nursery, can help you make decisions about the ongoing changes in your landscape. Whether you do the work yourself or hire someone, it's much easier to keep up with the maintenance than to try to undo years of neglect.

CHAPTER 3

COMPOSTING

In some areas, the soil is poor to average. Construction practices of clear-cutting trees and bulldozing away the topsoil have made the remaining soil too compacted and conditions too harsh for roots to grow. If you live in such an area, composting may help you regain what has been lost or depleted. It has the added benefit of reducing the amount of garbage we throw into our landfills.

Composting is an excellent way to recycle organic matter that can be used as a soil amendment or fertilizer. Its use has greatly increased with the popularity of organic farming. Composting can be as simple as forming a pile of leaves and other organic green material in a corner of the yard and turning it every so often. Or it can be done using more complicated systems that monitor temperature, moisture, oxygen, carbon, and other ingredients. Whichever route you take, it's hard to go wrong with composting, because it closely mimics what nature does, and the benefits are equally impressive.

There are many ingredients and methods to composting, but there are four main factors that are crucial: water, oxygen, nitrogen, and carbon. The availability of these four factors, along with the right ratio and timing, means the difference between success and failure. To put it simply, composting duplicates nature's technique of breaking down organic matter in order to unlock and recycle nutritional benefits into the soil to make them available for uptake by living root systems.

The heavy lifting in composting is performed by tiny microorganisms that are tasked with breaking down organic matter. Your goal as a good composter is to make the conditions right for these microorganisms to multiply and do their thing. This requires diligence on your part to ensure that water, oxygen, nitrogen, and carbon are not only available, but in the right ratios.

The process of composting uses a lot of oxygen and water as it produces heat and releases steam. Oxygen must be replaced through aeration; you achieve this by turning the compost frequently. You can purchase composting tumbling equipment, or you can turn compost the old-fashioned way, with a pitchfork. Water must be replenished periodically, either by rainfall or the garden hose.

Nitrogen- and carbon-rich organic matter is the key component of compost. The ratio of carbon to nitrogen should be at least two to one. Carbon comes from mulched wood, sawdust, corn, paper, ashes, pine needles, and dry leaves. Nitrogen-rich materials include fruit and vegetable scraps, grass, weeds, coffee grounds, chicken poop, and most green vegetation. This is not an exhaustive list, but it is a good place to start. The ingredients of compost must be organic. Do not add processed food scraps or meat.

Since the idea is to break down the nitrogen- and carbon-rich components, it works a lot faster if you shred the materials before adding them to the pile. It's also true that sticks, straw, and other coarse material can help keep the pile aerated. You may even give things a boost by purchasing compost bacteria from your local nursery and adding it to the mix.

Unless you've purchased a tumbling composter, start your pile directly on the dirt to attract worms and other natural composters, such as microorganisms. You can add compost ingredients directly to the pile on a regular basis by mixing them in rather than piling them on top.

Covering your compost will help prevent it from getting too soggy during torrential downpours. But do not cover it so tightly that it does not allow for air movement. Erecting a canopy a foot or so above it works well.

Once your yard waste and table scraps have turned into nutrient-rich compost, you can add it to your garden beds. You can also place a one-inch layer over your trees' root zones and then cover that with another inch or two of wood-chip mulch. Furthermore, an Air-Spade™ (a specialized tool that blows compressed air at an extremely high velocity) can be used to blend the compost into the trees' root zones prior to placing the wood-chip mulch on top.

Composting is a fun and productive way to enrich your landscape environment. I recommend you give it a try. You may be amazed at the results.

CHAPTER 4

GREEN, GREEN, THE GRASS IS GREEN!

Is THE GRASS REALLY GREENER on the other side of the fence? It just might be, but it does not have to be that way. Understanding a little more about the fundamentals of healthy grass can help you improve the quality of your lawn. After all, nice grass is healthy grass. But in becoming better educated about caring for your grass, beware of misconceptions and myths—some put forth by the people trying to sell you products or services.

Myth 1: You need to fertilize often with a high-nitrogen fertilizer.

Simply not true. Beware of those who might benefit from trying to convince you otherwise. Overfertilizing can cause far more problems than it solves. It makes the grass grow too fast, which often leads to disease and insect attack. Just as with trees, too much nitrogen-induced growth attracts nitrogen-loving pests that come to feed. Additionally, overfertilizing can have a negative effect on the surrounding environment. If you have cool-season grass (versus warm-season grass), you should avoid fertilizing when the grass is dormant or about to go dormant.

Myth 2: You should keep the grass cut low to avoid having to cut it as often.

As a general rule, keep the lawn mower set at its highest setting, and do not remove more than the top third. If you remove more than that, the grass becomes stressed and uses available resources in an effort to regenerate. Removing just the top third and allowing it to remain within the lawn lets valuable resources recycle back into the soil. Additionally, taller grass tends to shade out weeds, encourages root growth, and helps make the lawn drought tolerant.

Myth 3: You must water the grass every day.

As with trees, frequent, shallow watering trains roots to grow toward the surface and become susceptible to drought damage. Except in the case of new seeding, you should water once or twice a week but for longer periods of time. The idea is to get the water to the lower levels of the root system, several inches into the soil, to train roots to grow deeper.

Soil composition is one of the key components of a healthy, green lawn. You want to start out by enhancing the soil conditions in order to give roots the best opportunity to grow and thrive. Microorganisms, earthworms, organic matter, oxygen, and moisture are some of the components of healthy soil. Chemical fertilizers do little to enhance the ecosystem of the soil, and their heavy salt content can disrupt the normal functions of microorganisms and earthworms.

Healthy soil leads to a healthy root system. A healthy root system, with access to water, nutrients, and oxygen, leads to healthy grass. Again, as with trees, what happens in the ground is one of the most important factors leading to what happens above ground.

Fall is a great time to enhance the soil and improve growing conditions for the roots of your grass. The first step is to grab your thatcher or rake and give the lawn a good once-over. You want to remove any dead matting, moss, and other debris in the way of the healthy grass. This also helps loosen compaction at the top layer of soil.

The next step is to aerate the root system to help water penetration and allow the roots to breathe. This important step, if it's done right, can break up compaction farther into the ground. If you use a mechanical aerator, go over the lawn multiple times. If you do it by hand, you can use a pitchfork to penetrate deeper and lift the soil slightly to loosen it. Generally, the more you aerate, the better.

Test the soil to see if it's alkaline or acidic. You can hire a professional to test the soil, but it's not hard to do it yourself with a simple tester. Perhaps the best thing to do is send a soil sample to the local lab, because it will also make recommendations for amendments. Ideal pH soil conditions for most grass are between 6.5 and 6.8. If the soil is too alkaline, you can mix in some iron sulfate. If the soil is too acidic, you might need to add lime.

Weeds need to go. They fight for the same resources as grass, and the winner takes over the lawn. Although applying a weed killer is easiest, pulling them out by their roots is best. As mentioned earlier, taller, healthier grass tends to keep weed growth to a minimum. You can always hire neighborhood kids to attack them one by one.

If you have a major weed problem or your soil is compacted and of poor quality, you may want to do something drastic and replace what you have. Remove the top six inches or so of soil, and replace it with new. If you have a small area to deal with (townhouse or postage-stamp lawn), you can attempt this by hand. If you have a larger property, you may have to bring in big equipment to get the job done more efficiently. Again, this is extreme and, in most cases, unnecessary.

Fall is also a good time to add new seed to fill in the bald spots and grow a thicker lawn. It may be a good idea to mix in some topsoil first and then overseed with high-quality grass seed suited for your climate and shade conditions. Water just enough to make the ground moist but not so much that it washes away the seed.

CHAPTER 5

YOUR GARDEN: SPRING INTO SUMMER

Chapters 5, 6, and 7 were written by Shirley Street, Master of Landscape Architecture and International Society of Arboriculture–certified arborist. She is the former city arborist for the City of Falls Church, Virginia. She works with the public works engineers in the design and construction of bioretention facilities (rain gardens) and the Falls Church Public Utility Department's "Living Classroom" in McLean, Virginia. After thirty-four years of employment with the City of Falls Church, she retired in the summer of 2013 to expand her landscape design business. You can reach her studio by phone at 202-234-9622.

Culver's Root (Veroinicastrum virginicum)

Allow your native plant garden to move seamlessly from spring into summer without missing a beat for you or for the native wildlife that will benefit from the plants you may choose. In the mid-Atlantic region, for instance, a variety of trees, shrubs, and flowering perennials in whites and pastels can provide a welcome visual respite from the early onset of hot weather. When you use native plants, you are providing yourself with a garden that spans the seasons. As a bonus, you are also providing many of the region's native birds, butterflies, and other beneficial insects with the support needed for their very existence.

Design Tip for Planting Perennials

Be bold and plant in numbers. For all but the very largest perennials, plant several of the same kind, generally allowing eighteen inches from the center of one plant to the next (twelve to fifteen inches for smaller plants and two feet for plants that grow larger). Consider the distance from which you will be viewing your chosen plants and the context of the area in which you are placing them to create a strong statement with color and texture. Also consider that the wildlife you hope to attract will more likely be drawn to your plantings if they are massed.

The Plants

For the mid-Atlantic region, start your early summer (May into June) with a cooling combination of a white flowering fringe tree (*Chionanthus virginicus*) and a Virginia sweet spire (*Itea virginica*). Fringe tree is considered a large shrub or small tree for zones three to nine. Its growth is slow to moderate, and it performs best in sun or partial shade and moist, well-drained soil. Fringe trees mature to a height and width of twelve to twenty feet, depending on growing conditions. The luscious, creamy-white panicles, which hang four to eight inches long, are slightly fragrant. They are my first signal, as the weather turns warm, to find a good hammock!

In September and October, female fringe trees produce berries that are eaten by birds. The male tree, however, tends to have the most productive flowering. As fringe trees are propagated from seed, it is difficult for the nurseries to determine which sex they are selling, but either way, you will win by having a fringe tree in your garden. Use the fringe tree as a specimen in a naturalistic setting or in a mixed border along with shrubs, flowering perennials, and grasses. In a large space, multiple flowering fringe trees would be stunning! Fringe tree has proven tolerant to pollution, so even urban gardeners can enjoy this native tree that also offers yellow fall foliage.

Virginia sweet spire (*Itea virginica*) combines nicely with fringe tree as it, too, has drooping, smaller racemes of slightly fragrant white flowers from May to early July. Found in nature along streambeds, lake edges, and in floodplains, sweet spire prefers moist soils but will tolerate drier conditions. While this plant is slow to moderate in its rate of growth, it will spread by root suckers over time to form thickets. This tendency makes sweet spire useful for erosion control on moist slopes and as cover for wildlife. Birds will eat the dry fruit capsules and small seeds, and butterflies find the flowers useful for nectar. The slow spread of these shrubs can be kept in check by occasional pruning of the roots. The average mature height of this plant is four to six feet. The fall garden bonus of Virginia sweet spire is the spectacular scarlet foliage that persists on the plant for several weeks. A fairly sunny exposure will result in the best fall color for Virginia sweet spire.

Blue-eyed grass, *Sisyrinchinum angustifolium*, is another flowering plant that spans spring into summer. This is a low-growing perennial (twelve to eighteen inches tall) that performs well as a garden edging plant or along the garden path. A member of the iris family, the plant has starlike flowers that open late in the day atop clumps of grasslike foliage that remains attractive even after the flush of blooms has passed. Do not overmulch this plant or provide organic matter, because it prefers poor soils similar to those where it occurs naturally in damp fields, meadows, and shores. While blue-eyed grass prefers moist, well-drained soil, it does tolerate some drought once established. According to William Cullina of the New England Wild Flower Society, while individual plants are short-lived, new plants will develop around the adults, giving way to self-perpetuating plants that develop into thick stands in time. As for wildlife associated with blue-eyed grass, bees find the flowers useful.

Just as the flowers of the plants noted earlier begin to wane, the flowers of many other natives emerge and will carry interest in your garden further into the summer months. The spires of Culver's root (*Veronicastrum virginicum*) begin to develop in June or July to elegant proportions and continue to flower for a month to six weeks. Planted as an accent, in groups, or waterside, Culver's root is a striking, graceful plant that also works well as a cutting flower. The flowers are typically white—though pale pink and lavender forms can be found for gardens—and all reach heights of three to six feet. Culver's root performs best in moist soils. While a good show of flowers may not occur until the second year after planting, the multiple wispy flowers atop the candelabra-like structure of this plant are well worth the wait. Divisions of the root system can be made early in the spring or in the fall if each rootstock segment has a bud. The flowers of Culver's root are useful to butterflies and bees alike. Leave the stem standing over winter, because several beneficial hibernating insects may find cover there. The dried stalks of Culver's root will add visual interest to your garden in winter as well.

Many other native perennials emerge with vibrant colors in the summer and fall. Add some beautiful, new native plants to your garden. When you do so, your garden begins to support natural processes that have evolved in your area over a very long time. Keeping those processes going is critical to sustaining the health of a region's natural ecosystem, and you can be a part of that effort.

CHAPTER 6
GARDEN PATH PLANTINGS

Shirley Street, MLA, landscape designer, and ISA-certified arborist

WHETHER YOUR GARDEN SPACE IS large or small, placing plants in relation to a shady garden path takes some measure of planning to produce good results. Appropriate choices of plants and their arrangement can ease your maintenance and provide years of enjoyment in a seasonally changing landscape.

Featured Plant Selections

Plants that are expected to thrive between stepping-stones need to be tough and able to spread, such as *Sedum ternatum* or woodland sedum. When considering a plant for your garden, it is wise to look at the conditions where the plant grows naturally. This little gem of an evergreen ground cover has a preference for a moist but well-drained soil in a partly shady location. Occurring naturally in woodlands, *Sedum ternatum* may be found clinging to rocks on the sides of streams or on rocky outcrops above the stream. These conditions can be replicated in the home garden where the plants can be allowed to scramble over stones or tree roots, wherever they can find a bit of shade and a rocky, loamy soil.

The fleshy, succulent leaves of *Sedum ternatum* allow the plant to survive some periods of drought, which makes it a good choice for bioretention or rain gardens. Rain garden plants must endure both short periods of inundation and occasional drought in soils that are engineered for rapid draining. Rain garden plants do need supplemental water in times of drought, particularly as the plants are becoming established.

Attractive white, starlike (shaped in five points) flowers occur above the leaves of this ten-inch-tall sedum. Flowering occurs for about a month in April or May. The species benefits wildlife: bees are attracted to its nectar, and two butterfly species are known to use this plant as a host. Once established, your *Sedum ternatum* requires little or no maintenance.

Another low-growing native plant that serves well at the edge of a path is *Carex flaccosperma* or blue wood sedge. This clump-forming sedge has been recommended as a replacement for the nonnative and overplanted *Liriope*. This lovely sedge enjoys light shade and is adaptable to various soils and moisture levels, tolerating medium to dry conditions in shade or periods of greater moisture. These attributes make the blue woodland sedge another good choice for the rain garden. Cutting the leaves of your woodland sedge back by about one-third can provide a neat look close to your garden path. This perennial, too, is evergreen to semievergreen in the mid-Atlantic region, making for a nice year-round edge to your garden path.

With regard to wildlife benefits, the leaves of *Carex flaccosperma* serve as a host for several butterflies. The seeds produced in the spring are food for at least two species of birds. Birds also use the leaves for nesting material.

Plant Arrangement

At the time of planting, space your *Sedum ternatum* plants six inches apart. If you are placing these plants between stepping-stones, be sure to leave enough space between the stones to nestle the young plants.

While you may want taller growing plants, such as other flowering perennials, shrubs, or a wildflower mix, beyond the stepping-stone path, allow at least two to three feet of low-growing plants along both sides of the path to keep tall plants from flopping over the path.

For variety, you may want to add a band of *Carex flaccosperma* or woodland sedge, or another low-growing perennial. *Carex flaccosperma* grows six to ten inches tall and spreads twelve inches wide. Place these plants ten to twelve inches apart.

As you set out native plants, be aware that you are recreating ecosystems that will attract a variety of native songbirds as well as butterflies and other beneficial insects. Allowing space both for you to move through your garden and for those creatures who may find food or cover in the garden that you have made for them can be beneficial for all. Be aware that, in time, the plants of your native garden will distribute themselves in their own way. This is part of the pleasure of creating a native garden, one that evolves on its own. Your role as a steward of the land will be to ensure that nonnative, invasive plants do not overtake and displace the young native plants before they have a chance to fully establish themselves.

Both the *Carex flaccosperma* and the *Sedum ternatum* are installed as small plants, while the wildflower mix can be sown as seed. The wildflower area is mainly the annual cover crop that is allowing the native seed mix of forbs and grasses to emerge in the time each requires. It will likely take two to three years for the wildflower mix to mature fully. The soil of the rain garden is an engineered mix, very high in coarse sand, allowing for rapid drainage. The idea of placing stepping-stones in a rain garden came from a need to allow maintenance workers access to the plants (and weeds that might occur in the garden). This placement of stepping-stones also allows the public to more easily see and enjoy the plants, as well as the native creatures that will be attracted to the garden. You can do the same in your own garden!

CHAPTER 7
FALL PERENNIALS

Shirley Street, MLA, landscape designer, and ISA-certified arborist

IF YOU THINK COLOR IN the garden occurs only in the spring or high summer, it's time you discovered the variety of colors a selection of summer-to-fall flowering plants can provide. Do not let your autumn garden fade to brown long before frost takes hold; enjoy a last blast of color to remember in the winter months to come!

While expanding the weeks of enjoyment in your garden with herbaceous plants that will last into autumn, you will also be increasing infiltration and slowing the amount of storm-water runoff from your land. With every square foot of property that you convert from turf grass into ground-layer plantings, you are contributing to this important environmental goal. The efforts of local governments to reduce the volume of runoff, which can be so damaging to local watersheds, are assisted by individual homeowners who turn greater portions of their land over to ground-layer plantings along with trees and shrubs.

DESIGN/MAINTENANCE TIPS

By creating natural plant communities, you can also reduce maintenance needs as the features of your landscape evolve into a natural order. While mulching/composting your new plantings will be beneficial to installation during the first few years, your more naturalized areas will need less mulching over time. Plants in these more naturally designed areas will form their own mulch, saving you time and money. These overwintering remains of plants also provide food and shelter for a variety of wildlife.

Group your perennials using a minimum of three plants of the same kind in the smallest garden spaces to multiple plants in larger areas. Simplify the layout of your perennials by arranging them in a triangular pattern. This triangle becomes a dynamic shape that can create the illusion of movement in your garden. In time, many of the recommended perennials will move within and, perhaps, outside your garden, reseeding in places other than where you originally planted them.

Some of these movements might be interesting while other relocations might seem too aggressive, particularly if the aggressors overtake a slower-moving, desirable plant. In the latter case, just pluck them out, transplant them where you like, give them to friends, or simply toss them away. Weeds are less likely to move into areas where you have established stable plant communities. In time, woody plants, trees, and shrubs may move into your garden, giving you an opportunity to determine if you want the space to grow into a woodland state or to maintain your garden of flowering perennials by removing the "woodies." You will always need to watch for and remove invasive, nonnative, and undesirable plants as soon as they appear. Remember that the movement of desirable plants is part of the evolution of your ground layer to a more natural order. Over time, the results might be surprisingly beautiful!

CHAPTER 8
THE COOLING EFFECT OF TREES

TREES HAVE AN ENORMOUS POSITIVE effect on our environment. They are nature's air conditioners and can significantly lower energy consumption. According to the Sacramento Municipal Utility District website (www.smud.org), "Fully grown, properly placed trees can cut your home cooling costs by up to 40 percent." The website has a Tree Benefits Estimator that will calculate your energy savings in actual dollars.

The following quotes are found on the Arbor Day Foundation website (**www.arborday.org**):

"The net cooling effect of a young, healthy tree is equivalent to ten room-sized air conditioners operating twenty hours a day." —*US Department of Agriculture*

"If you plant a tree today on the west side of your home, in five years your energy bills should be 3 percent less. In fifteen years the savings will be nearly 12 percent." —*Dr. E. Greg McPherson, Center for Urban Forest Research*

Who hasn't sought the cooling shelter of a shade tree on a hot summer day? At my son's soccer games, whenever there's a shade tree on the sidelines, parents and other fans are seen finding valuable relief and protection from the sweltering heat under its broad branches.

Did you know that shade is not the only way trees cool you? They also give off moisture through a process called *transpiration*. The process of transpiration pulls water out of the soil, up the trunk, and out to the branches where it is released through small openings in the leaves called *stomata*. This moisture cools the surrounding air. A group of trees exponentially increases the cooling effect. Through transpiration, a tree moves nutrients and other necessary elements up its trunk to where they are needed.

Additionally, trees reduce the effects of heat reflection from buildings, parking lots, and roads. Buildings and parking areas that are not shaded by trees are always substantially warmer than those that are. Heat reflection magnifies temperatures in the local environment, raising the amount of energy needed to cool buildings. Air conditioners have to run longer, which in turn further heats the outside air.

CHAPTER 9

THE LIFE CYCLE OF TREES

TREES HAVE VARIOUS STAGES OF life, just like humans. Each stage has its own requirements to fit the tree's needs at that point in the life cycle.

A newborn or *seedling* typically starts out life as a seed or acorn. Planted by man or nature in the right soil, at the right depth, with a little water and warmth, it will soon sprout into a bouncing baby tree. Seedlings tend to grow rather quickly if the conditions are right, but this is one of the most vulnerable parts of the life cycle. Droughts, lawn mowers, and animals are all natural enemies. Due to these hazards and many others, only a small percentage of newborn trees progress beyond the seedling stage; therefore the care they need is mainly in the form of physical protection, along with the right amount of water and nutrients.

Trees grown in the nursery are often grafted onto the root system of a compatible tree. This is done either because the particular variety does not propagate from a seed or cutting or because it is a way to get a genetic duplicate of the tree. Grafting plant material does not have to be done at the root level; it can be done on stems or even along the trunk of an older tree. Trees grown in a nursery environment have a distinct advantage in survivability rates due to the expert physical care they receive.

Soon the seedling will grow into a *sapling*. Saplings have started to take root, and this is the size where most nursery stock is brought into the landscape. The trunk diameter is about an inch or larger at chest height. Saplings are not as defenseless as seedlings, but they are still vulnerable to threats that include competition from larger trees, poor weather, and animal or human damage. Saplings are generally not able to reproduce. This is an important time to developmentally prune young trees to ensure proper branch spacing and scaffolding, strong trunk taper, and a single dominant trunk (versus *codominant* trunks).

The next stage in the life cycle of a tree is *young maturity*. Young maturity is the point where the tree reproduces and flowers, and the tree is in a vigorous growth stage. As the young tree comes of age, this is when many of the benefits come to fruition such as shade, fruit production, screening, and noise reduction. Young mature trees should still be structurally pruned on a regular basis to ensure these benefits. This stage may require additional pruning that might include cutting back from buildings, lights, walkways, and the like. Additionally, weak, dying, diseased, and other problem branches should be removed. Trees may be in this stage for a few years or many decades, depending upon the species.

A large, mature chestnut oak

When a tree enters an *older maturity* stage, it may still have many years of valuable life left in it. It may start to lose lower branches that are shaded out by the upper canopy. It is now quite large and has often become a prominent feature within the landscape, offering both beauty and shade. Regular pruning will help keep it healthy by removing dead and other problem branches, as mentioned earlier. Additionally, the mature tree might be a candidate for lightning protection to reduce the risk of a catastrophic strike. Installing a lightning protection system can be expensive due to the amount of labor involved and the high cost of copper, so this option is usually reserved for particularly valuable specimens within the landscape. Roots may grow as far as two to three times the diameter of the canopy (or drip line) in mature trees, so protecting them from compaction and competition from sod for water and nutrients becomes increasingly important. A two- to three-inch layer of wood-chip mulch out to the drip line will go a long way toward alleviating both of these problems. Additionally, mulch has the advantage of recycling nutrients back into the soil as the wood chips break down.

Eventually most trees will reach the point of decline. This may happen for some species after only a couple of decades, usually due to the trees' inherent structural problems. Bradford pears, for instance, tend to outgrow themselves and may start to break apart at about twelve to fifteen years of age. Other fast-growing species, such as Leyland cypress, may simply grow too big for their structure to withstand the next heavy ice storm. But for other species, including the bristlecone pine or the giant sequoia, the start of decline may not happen for several millennia. When decline does eventually begin, the tree may still hang on for a long time. Sometimes a top will blow out in a storm or other disaster, but the lower part of the tree still remains viable. These old, decrepit trees may remain for a generation or more, but eventually they will succumb to disease or physical damage and will die. But the story is not over just yet. As these trees decay and fall apart, they recycle nutrients back into the soil and become a source for new life.

CHAPTER 10

THE AMAZING LEAF!

WHAT'S NOT TO LIKE ABOUT fall? It's that time of year when football is in full swing, the kids are back in school, and the holiday season is just around the corner. And trees are showing off their beautiful colors!

Have you ever wondered what brings out the fall color of leaves? To find the answer, you have to understand a little bit about how trees and leaves work. Trees need to eat, just like you and I do, but, to dispel a myth, their food is not fertilizer any more than a multivitamin is food for us. Carbohydrates and sugars are the tree's real foods. Leaves produce carbohydrates and sugars through a process known as *photosynthesis*.

Start your recipe for photosynthesis with chlorophyll, a green substance contained within a plant's chloroplast. Stir in a little energy from sunlight, mix in some water and carbon dioxide, and you've whipped up a batch of carbohydrates and sugars—tree food. Chlorophyll is broken down during the process of photosynthesis, but new chlorophyll is produced to replace it during the growing season.

As summer transitions to fall and the weather cools, the flow of green chlorophyll is slowly cut off as the veins in the leaf close, especially at night. The lack of green chlorophyll reveals the true color pigments of the leaf that were hidden during the time of energy production. The process is a little more complicated than that, but those are the important highlights.

Why do trees lose their leaves in the fall? For one thing, if they did not, we would have to change the name of the season to something else. It's amazing how trees truly reflect the change of seasons more visually than perhaps anything else. But to answer the question, there are several compelling reasons trees lose their leaves. One reason is the potential damage to the structural integrity of branches that would be caused by heavy snow and ice clinging to leaves. Another is the loss of water that takes place during the process of transpiration—the movement of water from the root system, up the trunk and branches, and out through little openings, called stomata, in the leaves. Transpiration is important during energy production, but as sunlight becomes less available during the winter, photosynthesis stops. Ever so competent with their resources, trees stop the loss of water as much as possible.

As leaves fall to the ground, they form a protective layer over the tree's root system that regulates soil temperature, traps moisture, and alleviates compaction. As the leaves decay, vital nutrients are added to the soil and absorbed by the root system, completing a highly efficient natural cycle. Of course, we humans sometimes disrupt those benefits; we break out our rakes and spend hours of hard work removing every last leaf so that we can have the cleanest yard in the neighborhood. We experience some benefits, such as exercise, and the kids get to jump in the big pile of leaves. But raking is not good for the trees; if you let the leaves stay in place, you can help the process of decay and of recycling nutrients back into the soil. Go over the leaves with a mulching lawn mower a couple times, or throw them through a mulching chipper if you happen to have one handy. Chopping the leaves helps them decay much faster, which brings their benefits into play sooner.

Leaves also can help you identify trees. Start with a leaf's general shape and color, and look at its margins. Are the margins smooth, serrated, lobed, or serrated *and* lobed? Their appearance on the stem serves as a clue. They can be alternate or opposite along the stem, or they might be simple or compound.

There are books and interactive tools that will help you until you get to the right species. If you have an iPhone or iPad, the Leafsnap app can be downloaded for free. It's an app created by Columbia University, the University of Maryland, and the Smithsonian Institution that enables you to take a picture of a leaf and then identifies the tree for you. Beware: it has mixed reviews because it does not always seem to work correctly, but it is free. The alternative is to obtain a tree identification book and do it the old-fashioned way.

So enjoy the colors of fall this autumn, but with a better understanding of the wonder of leaves. You can simply admire them from a distance, use them for enhancing the soil, or play in a big pile of them. They are beautiful, yet highly functional!

CHAPTER 11
TREE SELECTION AND PLANTING TIPS

ARE YOU THINKING OF PLANTING a tree this spring? It's a good idea; you'll enjoy many benefits that can last for generations. Trees provide beauty in the landscape, clean air, shade from the summer sun, screening for privacy, and even peace of mind. However, those benefits won't last long if you don't start things off the right way. With a little planning, you can avoid many of the problems that might hamper your efforts.

It's always good to start by selecting the right tree for the location you have chosen. It sounds so simple; yet as arborists, we see many trees in the landscape that should never have been planted where they are. The following questions will help you narrow down your list of possible choices.

Let's begin with the general purpose of the tree. Do you need screening for privacy? How about wind reduction or shade? Or perhaps you would like a prominent landscape feature, in which case you should consider the tree's shape, color, flowers, and overall size.

What about site conditions? Is the planting area saturated or dry most of the time? How much sunlight or shade is present? Will it be an understory tree, or will it have plenty of room to grow? Picture in your mind the mature size of the tree. You don't want it to crowd out other important landscape features.

You should also plant a wide variety of species in your landscape. Native species are usually a good choice, because they have naturally adapted to the local climate and conditions. Additionally, native trees are more likely to be resistant to pest and disease problems. All of these and more are considerations to keep in mind when selecting your new tree.

A common problem is to overplant with just a few species. This limits the number of beneficial predators that feed on harmful pests. If you overplant with any particular species, your landscape is vulnerable to devastation by a disease or pest infestation. Follow the 30-20-10 percent rule of selection advocated by the late Dr. Frank Santamour, the former geneticist at the National Arboretum in Washington DC. Don't plant more than 30 percent from any plant family. Additionally, don't choose more than 20 percent from any genera or use more than 10 percent of plants from a specific species. Sticking to this rule will help ensure you have a wide variety of plants in your landscape.

Once you've settled on the type of tree to plant, it's time for a visit to the nursery to pick one out. Take a good look at leaf color and size along with branch structure. You want to avoid broken, crossing, rubbing, and of course, dead and dying branches. Cracks or sunscald may be indicators of more serious problems along the trunk. And don't forget to look below for girdling and circling roots that can choke off the vascular system as the tree matures. Note that the original planting depth in the nursery can be critical to the future health of the tree. You should be able to see a root flare at the point where the trunk meets the soil.

Believe it or not, if you plant a smaller tree (three to five feet tall) versus a larger tree (seven to nine feet tall), the smaller tree will often be larger than the bigger one within about five to seven years. This is because a smaller tree will tend to have more of its original root system intact at the time of planting and will adapt to the surrounding soil better. Larger trees tend to suffer from planting shock and can take several years to recover. An added benefit of planting a smaller tree is that the smaller tree is not only easier to transport and plant, it's also less expensive.

You have your tree; now let's get it planted. To give the new tree the best chances for long-term survival, dig the planting hole at least twice the width of the root ball, but leave a pedestal for the root ball to sit on. The top of the root ball should be a couple of inches higher than the surrounding ground level. Remember the old adage: "Plant them high, and they never die; plant them low, and they never grow."

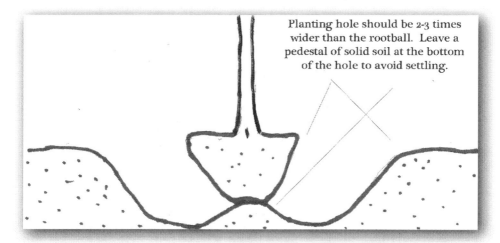

Planting hole should be 2-3 times wider than the rootball. Leave a pedestal of solid soil at the bottom of the hole to avoid settling.

Arborists recommend using only the existing soil as backfill. In other words, don't use amendments. Remove any wire baskets, burlap (even if it's biodegradable), ropes, and the like. If necessary, stake the tree outside the root ball (for example, if the tree has a thick canopy). If you use stakes, remove them after one year. The tree will develop a stronger trunk and have a nice taper if it is allowed to move freely with the wind.

Finally, apply a two- to three-inch layer of wood-chip mulch. Keep the mulch away from the trunk. Spread it as far out over the future root system as possible. Whatever you do, don't pile it up "volcano" style. Plant trees together in shared mulch beds or tree islands, but be sure to allow room for mature growth.

Follow these guidelines, and you will have a tree with far fewer health problems in the future.

CHAPTER 12
THE IMPORTANCE OF GOOD SOIL

SOIL IN THE URBAN ENVIRONMENT is subject to many factors that limit its ability to provide the proper nutrients, moisture, and structure necessary for healthy trees in the landscape. Compaction, lack of organic material, insufficient pore space, and other critical problems conspire to make a harsh environment for root systems. During construction, topsoil is scraped away, natural grades are changed, and the soil environment is radically altered. Additionally, grass is in fierce competition for available water and tends to absorb most of the moisture before it has a chance to reach the trees' root systems.

A healthy tree requires a properly functioning root system, which in turn must be located within a healthy soil ecosystem. This living ecosystem requires many key elements coming together, often in symbiotic relationships. A primary ingredient is organic matter, which breaks down over time to provide many nutrients needed by the tree. Organic matter provides a habitat for the required microorganisms, worms, and other living organisms. It is also necessary to have plenty of open-pore space within the soil for the storage of oxygen and water.

How do you enhance the soil surrounding your tree's root system? Fortunately, there are new tools and procedures that allow arborists to do just that. The Air-Spade actually removes soil from the root systems without damaging the roots. Originally developed to safely uncover land mines, the Air-Spade has been proven in numerous university studies to safely blow soil from roots with a supersonic blast of air, without damaging the roots.

CHAPTER 13
MULCH FOR YOUR TREES

MULCH HAS MANY POSITIVE BENEFITS for the health of your trees. Trees in the forest produce a large volume of mulch naturally but can rarely do so effectively in the urban environment. Leaves, twigs, branches, and other organic matter drop to the forest floor and recycle nutrients back into the soil over the root zone. Soil in the forest contains the nutrients and organisms that are essential for optimum tree health.

Good soil contains much more than just the proper level of nutrients. Good soil has to function properly. There is an important balance or *ecosystem* that works to keep the soil operating correctly. The process starts with a good source of organic matter. That organic matter is broken down by organisms that include, among other things, worms and microorganisms. Deteriorating organic matter naturally aerates the soil, which helps to alleviate soil compaction. It also releases available nitrogen for easy absorption by the root system.

Good soil also contains *mycorrhizae.* Mycorrhiza is a naturally occurring fungus that attaches to absorbing root hairs in a symbiotic relationship. It spider-webs out into the surrounding soil, increasing the absorbing capability of the root hairs by up to one hundred times. The natural mulching process in the forest is the ideal habitat for mycorrhizae to thrive.

Mulch helps to retain moisture in the soil during droughts. It also regulates soil temperature, keeping roots at the proper temperature throughout the year. It reduces mechanical damage to roots and trunks from lawn mowers and weed whackers. These devices often cut through the bark into the vascular system, disrupting the vascular flow of water and nutrients. The cuts also become openings for pests and diseases to breach natural defenses and attack the tree.

As beneficial as mulch is, improper mulching can be worse than no mulch at all. Initially, mulch should be spread in a two- to three-inch layer over the root zone, but it should not come in contact with the root flare. Such contact can cause moisture to become trapped against the trunk, which can lead to trunk rot and create the perfect environment for harmful insects to flourish in close proximity to the trunk.

The tree on the left was buried under "volcano" style mulching, while the trees on the right have the mulch spread out in a thin, but wide layer.

Wood-chip mulch is much better than the commercially available, double-shredded mulch. Wood-chip mulch is larger and heavier. It breaks down more slowly, so it lasts longer. Double-shredded mulch can mat down and create an impermeable glaze that keeps water from penetrating into the soil.

A new layer of mulch can be added every year or so, but only one to two inches deep, depending on how much remains from the previous application. The old mulch should be turned with a hard rake first and then the new layer spread on top.

Adding chemical fertilizers helps very little in rebuilding a depleted soil structure. Chemical fertilizers can also cause nutrient imbalances, causing more problems than they solve. What is more, they often increase the salt content within the soil, which can actually draw moisture away from absorbing roots.

CHAPTER 14

FERTILIZING

ARE YOUR TREES LOOKING A little peaked? It might be that they just need some nutrition. Urban soils are often depleted of the nutrients that are found naturally in the forest, and trees have a harder time absorbing what is there. There are several factors that can lead to this condition:

- Competition from sod
- Elimination of natural sources of recycled nutrients like leaves and twigs
- Soil compaction
- Limitations on root-zone size
- Removal of topsoil during a construction process

Fertilizing trees has sometimes been a controversial subject. In the past, high-nitrogen fertilizers often caused more problems than they solved. Too much nitrogen fertilizer leads to increased nitrogen-induced sucker growth that, in turn, attracts nitrogen-sucking insects.

You may notice some of the signs that a tree is suffering from low levels of soil nutrients. These include slow growth of leaves, shoots, and trunk, along with overall reduced size and discoloration of leaves. Dead branches, *dieback* from the tips of branches, and problems with insect attacks and disease may also be indicators of a lack of nutrients. A soil test can help determine if there are any deficiencies.

The best solution is to rebuild the soil structure in a manner that mimics what is found naturally in the forest. To this end, a two- to three-inch layer of wood-chip mulch placed over the root system adds a source of nutrients as it breaks down over time. However, sometimes mulch is not applied correctly, even when it is installed by professional landscape companies. There are also more intensive methods for improving soil structure that have much faster results.

Rebuilding soil can also cause conflict because property owners sometimes don't want to remove sod and replace it with wood-chip mulch for aesthetic reasons. However, to reduce the competition between grass and tree roots, it helps to have a defined border of mulch as far out to the tree's drip (or canopy) line as possible.

Fertilizing can help replenish missing nutrients, if done correctly. It's best done down at the root level, with deep-root injection, for the same reason we recommend longer, penetrative watering. This encourages roots to flourish at lower levels in the soil, rather than remaining shallow and growing toward the surface. Additionally, deep-root fertilizing reaches down to where the majority of roots are located within the soil.

Slow-release fertilizer with lower concentrations of nitrogen and phosphorus is much better than the high-nitrogen fertilizers used in the past. It should also contain the micronutrients and trace minerals necessary for good tree health. Slow release makes the nutrients available over a much longer period of time, to be absorbed when the trees need them most. When appropriate, a good, well-balanced fertilizer suitable for your particular trees will go a long way toward keeping them healthy over time and will help reduce attacks from pests and diseases.

CHAPTER 15
PLANT YOUR CHRISTMAS TREE!

Plant your Christmas tree and have a keepsake for years to come.

Do YOU WANT TO REMEMBER this Christmas for many years to come? Would you like to help the environment at the same time? Then consider planting your Christmas tree after the holidays. Read on to learn how to do it the right way.

Start by choosing the right tree species; examples are Norway spruce, white pine, blue spruce, Scotch pine, Douglas fir, and cedar, among others. Study the space you have available inside as well as the planting location outside. Select a tree that will fit well in both places.

It's easier to deal with a smaller tree, especially when you take into consideration the weight of the root ball. It's best to buy a tree with the root ball wrapped in burlap from a local nursery or tree farm. Be sure to handle it with care during transport to avoid damaging the root ball. Once you get the tree inside, place it in a galvanized bucket, and use a few large rocks to prop it up. Leave the burlap intact, and put mulch in the bucket around the root ball to prevent it from drying out.

Predig the planting hole, because the ground may be frozen after the holidays in January. Choose a location that is protected from wind, preferably behind an existing evergreen tree. Dig the planting hole at least twice the width of the root ball, but leave a pedestal for the root ball to sit on. Place the dirt on a tarp or in a wheelbarrow, and then bring it into the garage, shed, or other shelter. Put straw in the planting hole to keep it from freezing.

While it is indoors, situate the tree away from sources of heat and dry air, such as fireplaces, kitchens, or air ducts, and be sure to avoid direct sunlight. Instead of watering the traditional way, a better way that helps prevent damage caused by overwatering is to place ice cubes on top of the root ball. As the ice melts, water slowly becomes available to the roots. Avoid leaving stagnant water, which may cause root decay, in the bucket. Additionally, spray the tree with an antidesiccant to help keep the needles from drying out.

Be careful when placing lights and ornaments on the branches so you avoid damaging delicate tissue. Use low-wattage lights, and drape them gently over the branches.

After the holidays, avoid shocking the tree by slowly adapting it to the outside climate. Bring it into your garage or place it by a sheltered, outside wall for a couple of weeks. If the prevailing winds in your area generally come from the west, for example, then an eastern wall is probably the best place. If the tree starts out in the garage, move it to a sheltered, outside wall for another week or two. Keep an eye on the long-range weather forecast. If there's going to be a period of mild weather, plant the tree immediately.

During planting, remove the burlap from the trunk and root ball. Position the tree in the hole you dug earlier, and replace with the dirt you previously dug up and stored in the garage.

In future years, you and your family can decorate your outside Christmas tree with lights, for added Christmas cheer.

CHAPTER 16

WINTER TREE CARE

THE FRIGID WINDS OF WINTER can be harsh to your trees. Snow and ice may add to the threat as heavy weight accumulates on branches. Trees in the urban environment often don't have much protection from severe environmental conditions. Is there anything you can do to help ensure their survival into spring?

There are no guarantees, but the best protection is a healthy, structurally sound tree. However, before we delve into what you can do to reduce winter tree damage, keep in mind that there are differences, due to their growing environments, between how trees in the forest and their urban cousins overwinter. Trees in the forest tend to be protected from the elements by their greater numbers, whereas trees in an urban environment are often growing by themselves out in the open, with little protection and support.

Damaging wind shear is reduced as it enters a forest. Trees growing along the edge of the forest that faces the prevailing winds tend to have stronger root systems and trunk flares that help compensate for the extra force they encounter. Evergreens, which are often located along the transition between open areas and the forest, also help dissipate the force of wind. Trees in an urban location might be alone in a yard, with nothing to block strong winds.

In the forest, the weight of snow and ice is spread out over many branches at varying levels, lessening the impact on any particular branch. In the urban landscape, a lone tree must take on the full weight, which can cause stress cracks or breakage. Keep in mind that small cracks can grow into larger ones that may not become apparent until many months later. This is one reason you might see a "healthy-looking" branch suddenly break off on a windless day.

After a heavy snowstorm, you may notice some of your trees bending over or "touching their toes" due to the heavy weight of the snow. This tends to happen to evergreens, particularly Leyland cypress. Take a broom or long pole and gently brush the snow off the branches to reduce the weight of the snow. If the trunk or branches are not broken, they will often go back to their original shape.

Soil conditions are normally better in the forest. This is because leaves that fall are allowed to decay on the forest floor, creating thick, rich topsoil. Deeper topsoil encourages roots to grow both downward and outward. The deeper roots are able to grow, the better the stabilization of the tree. Conversely, urban soils can be of poor quality, causing roots to pancake out instead of growing downward, thereby creating less stability. Better soil conditions make for healthier trees that are more able to withstand brutal winter conditions. A two- to three-inch layer of wood-chip mulch over the root system can duplicate many of the benefits found in the forest floor. Mulch helps to regulate harsh winter temperatures over the roots.

Give your trees a drink this winter. Trees go dormant, but that doesn't mean they're dead (at least, I hope not). All living organisms need water to survive, and trees are no different. If temperatures rise above freezing, and the ground is dry because it hasn't rained or snowed, by all means, give them a good watering, just as you would during a summer drought.

One of the most damaging aspects of winter can be the salt that humans pile in large quantities over the soil above the roots of trees located near roads, parking lots, sidewalks, and driveways. Salt draws moisture away from the roots and can lead to the same health symptoms that are produced by droughts. Avoid using salts to melt ice on your walkways and driveway. If road salt gets anywhere near your trees or plants, remove it as quickly as possible before the snow and ice melt. If you suspect that salt has been introduced into the soil, the best course of action is to dilute it with large quantities of water as soon as is practical.

Contrary to popular belief, dormancy is actually one of the best times to prune most species of trees. Winter is an excellent time to structurally prune trees because the branching structure is easily seen when no leaves impede the overall view. Structural pruning helps make the trunk stronger and the tree less likely to sustain damage from storms. Young trees in particular need structural or developmental pruning, but mature trees can also benefit. Dead branches and those that are diseased, decayed, dying, crossing and rubbing, or overcrowded should be removed from the crown or canopy.

Trees that are at risk for snow or ice damage may benefit from having cabling and bracing hardware installed to reinforce weak junctures. Trees with more than one major trunk may be at risk of splitting apart from the added weight of snow and ice, especially when wind is added to the equation. Keep in mind that not all trees are candidates for this procedure.

You can certainly reduce the risk of damage from the harsh weather; however, you can never completely eliminate risk. The care discussed here can go a long way toward helping your trees survive or even thrive through the winter.

CHAPTER 17
WATER YOUR TREES THIS SUMMER

How long could you last without water? Do you think you could go for a few days or maybe a week? Although we tend not to think about it much, trees also need water. In fact, they need it every bit as much as we do. A host of tree health problems are initially due to lack of water.

Every living cell within a tree must have water to function, just as we do. Cells that lack water soon die. Additionally, the tree's vascular system uses water to transport nutrients and perform other vital operations.

Trees absorb moisture from the ground. That moisture then moves from the root system to the trunk and, from there, moves to the branches and leaves. It is then emitted from small openings in the leaves to complete a process called transpiration. Transpiration helps keep trees cool in the hot summer sun. This is why being in the shade of a tree will cool you more than being in the shade of manmade structures.

Because trees obtain their water mostly from the ground, it's important to know how things work. The ground holds moisture within open-pore space. Poor, compacted soil has very little open-pore space available, so rainwater tends to run off. Organic matter, including wood-chip mulch, increases pore space within the soil and reduces evaporation at the surface level.

How much is enough? Large, well-established trees should be watered deeply every four to six days during droughts. Smaller, younger trees should be watered every two to four days. Deep watering on a less frequent basis trains trees to become more drought resistant. Frequent, shallow watering will train roots to grow toward the surface, where they are less effective and more prone to become damaged by prolonged periods of drought. Additionally, they are more likely to be mechanically injured.

So give your trees a nice long drink of water at the rates we've discussed here. Watering your trees is crucial to their good health. Your trees will not only be healthier, you will enjoy them more and spend less money trying to nurse them back to health.

CHAPTER 18
EIGHT SIGNS OF TROUBLE WITH YOUR TREES

As with people, when problems affect the health of your tree, early detection can often mean the difference between life and death. Signals of impending trouble are sometimes obvious, but at other times, you may need to make a closer inspection. Because trees are living organisms, you should keep an eye out for abnormalities on a regular basis. The following list of eight signs of trouble is by no means exhaustive, but it's a good way to start.

1. **Small leaves**, especially high up in the canopy, may be an indication that water is not reaching the upper branches. Underlying causes may be root or soil problems, vascular damage within the trunk or branches, pests, drought, or other issues. Additionally, when water intake is a problem, leaves will tend to droop or flag downward.
2. **Leaf color and damage.** Look for deep, vivid color in the leaves. Pale or off-color leaves might be a sign of pest or disease damage, too much or too little water, or lack of nutrition or sunlight. Damage by insects, especially some leaf-sucking pests, can result in a spider-web look to the leaves. Leaf-chewing insects tend to leave holes.

The large root girdling on this tree will eventually cut off the flow of water and nutrients.

3. **Girdling or circling roots** can eventually choke the tree's vascular system, cutting off necessary water and nutrients to the canopy. Watch for evidence of belowground girdling roots when you can't see the normal root flare. Depending on the size of the girdling root, pruning it may be an option. Girdling roots are often the result of improper planting: trees should not go straight into the ground like telephone poles –the base should flair outward as it enters the ground.

Large vertical cracks can be a signal of impending tree failure.

4. **Stress cracks** in the trunk (or branches) can be a sign of serious structural weakness. It is especially grave if the crack opens and closes as the tree sways in the wind. The part of the tree above the crack is vulnerable to failure. Stress cracks can be caused by a number of factors, including severe wind, heavy canopy growth, and weak unions.
5. **Fungi** may appear on the leaves, branches, trunk, or roots. Mushrooms on the trunk, branches, or roots can often indicate internal decay. Fungus on the ground near the trunk points to a high likelihood of root decay. An arborist certified in pest control may be able to treat some fungi problems, depending upon the severity and condition.
6. **Branch tip dieback,** or tree demise that proceeds from the most external areas inward, may be due to root or soil problems, vascular damage in the trunk, lack of nutrients, pests, drought, or other issues. Proper diagnosis is vital to alleviate this issue. Once the cause is isolated and the condition arrested, the dieback can be pruned out.
7. **Late leaf development or early leaf drop** is an indication that the tree is under stress. It is important to properly diagnose the cause and initiate recommended treatments promptly.
8. **Pests and diseases** can cause havoc with the health of your trees. If diagnosed early enough, most can be controlled. The best defense is a healthy tree. These invaders tend to attack trees that are already under stress.

Trees in the urban landscape must deal with a number of factors not found in their natural environment. These may include lack of organic matter available for decomposition into the root system, heat from nearby buildings and parking lots, lack of nearby trees for cooling and protection, compacted soil, competition from grass, limited areas for root growth, and other sources of stress. Because the best defense is a healthy tree, create an environment for your tree that mimics its natural environment. See chapter 20, "Urban Tree Stress," for more information on these issues.

CHAPTER 19
LET'S GET TO THE ROOT OF THE PROBLEM

Crossing roots can cause problems as they grow.

THERE IS A REASON WE say, "Get to the root of the problem." The least visible part of a tree has an enormous effect on the health of the tree parts you can see. Roots are often the most overlooked, neglected, and abused component of the tree's anatomy. Root problems are a major contributor to tree health issues in general.

Contrary to popular belief, roots are located mostly in the top six to ten inches of soil. This is the case in the mid-Atlantic region, for example. Due to the abundance of clay and rock, there is not a deep layer of topsoil; consequently, roots will "pancake" out horizontally rather than grow downward. Believe it or not, roots can often extend two to four times the diameter of the tree's drip line (the area below the canopy, or branches, of the tree).

Roots perform several critical functions for trees. They provide structural stability by literally keeping tons of trunk and canopy upright. They also absorb the necessary water, nutrients, and oxygen that every living cell and tissue within the tree must have in order to survive and function. Clearly, without a healthy root system, the tree cannot be healthy.

As vital as they are to the health and survival of trees, roots are often the victims of mostly unintended but sometimes severe abuse. They may be forced to grow in a space that is far too confined for the size of the tree. They are often cut, compacted, drowned, starved, and poisoned; damaged by lawn mowers, weed whackers, cars, and construction crews; and otherwise abused in the urban setting. It seems that because they are mostly out of sight, they are mostly out of mind, and we don't consider their importance while we are performing other tasks.

If we take a good look at how roots grow naturally in the forest, we can begin to see why they have such a hard time in urban environments. Conditions are far more challenging outside of the forest, resulting in different levels in the health and growth of the root systems.

Soil conditions in the forest are significantly better. Leaves and twigs are allowed to decay where they fall, thus recycling nutrients and organic matter back into the soil. Therefore, over time, topsoil tends to become deep and rich. The forest floor is alive with microorganisms, earthworms, and *mycorrhizae* (a symbiotic root fungus that increases root absorption). The physical structure of the soil also allows oxygen into open-pore space where it can be absorbed easily by roots.

Forest trees share root zones and available resources.

Trees growing in groups, as we see in the forest, often share resources. Their roots live in a symbiotic relationship, and they are able to share water and nutrients. Urban trees tend to grow by themselves, with their root systems covered by a thick and unyielding layer of grass that competes for available water and nutrients.

In the urban environment, soil conditions are harsh and hardly conducive to healthy root growth and function. Compaction squeezes out open-pore space, thereby reducing available oxygen and water levels. Leaves and twigs are removed so they are unable to add organic matter back into the soil. In fact, during new construction, topsoil is usually removed, and the original grading is drastically changed. Everything from soil ecosystems to water flow is affected. Additionally, grading often removes large portions of root systems.

Roots provide stability to trees. They spider-web out into the soil as they attach to rocks, crevices, and whatever else they can in order to hold the rest of the tree upright. Considering how much stress is caused by the force of heavy winds that can catch thick canopies like a sail, it is amazing that roots are able to keep trees upright. This ability is greatly reduced in cut, diseased, or damaged roots.

Root diseases that include *Armillaria* (also known as shoestring root rot), other forms of root rot, vascular wilts, and various pathogens can cause considerable damage to roots. Because they exist mostly below ground, these problems can be hard to see and diagnose. Severe cases can sometimes be seen above ground. Tools such as the Air-Spade are now available to help the arborist expose and view the root system without causing damage to it. The Air-Spade also allows poor, compacted soil to be replaced with nutrient- and mineral-rich organic soil amendments.

Root problems are sometimes caused by improper planting. Root girdling, which may be caused by burlap that was left around the root ball or by soil amendments added during planting, can eventually choke off a tree's vascular system by causing roots to grow in a circular pattern around the root ball. Additionally, planting a tree too deep often makes it hard for new roots to grow into the surrounding soil. Deep planting can result in unsuitable, adventitious roots growing from the side of the trunk rather than from the root flare, where desirable roots grow.

A two- to three-inch layer of wood-chip mulch spread out over the root system can have many advantages, but only if it's applied correctly. Mulch should never come into contact with the trunk and should not be piled up "volcano" style. Wood-chip mulch is the recommended mulch to use because it breaks down naturally and controls weeds better. Double-shredded mulch can glaze over, which creates an impermeable barrier that prevents water from reaching the roots below. Wood-chip mulch protects roots from mechanical damage from lawn mowers, regulates soil temperatures, and holds moisture in the root zone. Spread it over the root system as far as practical. Try to go as far as the drip line of the canopy, and you'll go a long way toward alleviating the competition problem created by sod over the root system.

CHAPTER 20
URBAN TREE STRESS

This chapter was written by Brandon Gallagher Watson, communication director and ISA arborist for Rainbow Treecare Scientific Advancements. The pictures were provided by the author.

URBAN TREE STRESS IS A widely accepted term that describes the factors that lead to urban trees typically living significantly shorter lives than trees growing in natural settings. As the name implies, urban tree stress affects trees growing in urban environments where conditions are not necessarily conducive to proper tree growth.

Urban tree stress can be diagnosed by recognizing a number of different symptoms brought on by a variety of causes. Unlike, for instance, a vascular wilt disease—where one can pinpoint a susceptible host, a specific pathogen, a suitable environment for infection, and often a single treatment option—urban tree stress is not as easy to put into a box. As such, its management almost always requires a multifaceted approach.

Why Are Trees in Urban Landscapes at Risk?

To understand how trees become susceptible to stress, it is first necessary to understand how trees grow in their native environments. Like all living things, trees have adapted themselves over millions of years to thrive in certain conditions. Every tree requires a specific soil texture, nutrient complex, stand density, moisture regimen, temperature range, photo period, and associated organisms (soil microorganisms, beneficial insects, etc.) to reach its full genetic potential. Needless to say, when a tree is taken from an environment that is the result of millions of years of adaptation and is planted in, say, a downtown sidewalk box, one or more of its requirements will inevitably be compromised. This places stress on the tree, and subsequently it may not thrive.

One way to understand the impact of urban tree stress is through the roles of fungal diseases and aggressive insects such as bark beetles and borers, which are vital in a native ecosystem. These organisms help maintain the health of a tree population by "thinning the herd" of weakened individuals, and they often have no effect on a healthy tree. Many tree pests that are minor issues in a native setting become major pests for city trees, however, when urban tree stress has made them susceptible.

What Else Causes Urban Tree Stress?

Urban tree stress can be caused by one or more contributing factors, and each species of tree varies in its inherent ability to resist these factors. The factors that create these difficult growing situations for the tree include competing turf grass, compacted and nutrient-poor soils, too little or too much water, temperatures that are too hot or too cold, pollution, improper planting, and eventually being too large for the planting site. Age also plays a contributing role in the susceptibility to stress; newly planted trees and older, mature individuals are the most likely trees to be negatively affected. Root loss from construction damage, grade changes, or transplanting can be a significant source of stress for all trees. Trees such as ash, ginkgo, Chinese pistache, Bradford pear, and hackberry are well known for their hardiness in urban landscapes because they thrive even in difficult growing situations. But the more negative factors a tree faces, the more difficult it will be for that tree to survive. This is true even for the hardiest of species.

Symptoms a tree may express when suffering from urban tree stress will differ by species, age of the tree, and source of the stress. Typical symptoms of tree stress include stunted growth, epicormic sprouts, scorched leaves, and chlorosis. Other visual indicators may include frost cracks, cankers, decay, and the presence of insect pests, especially borers and bark beetles. An increase in fruit production can also be a signal. Trees that sense their own decline will often increase reproductive structures as a last-ditch survival effort. Other symptoms that may not be as readily seen are root decline and infection by root-rot diseases such as Armillaria.

Can Urban Tree Stress Be Managed?

Urban trees growing in a parking lot

When it comes to a management plan for confronting urban tree stress, an ounce of prevention is worth a metric ton of cure. Avoiding sources of stress is significantly easier and cheaper than trying to remediate them after a tree has begun to show symptoms of decline. Certainly, getting a tree properly established by ensuring the tree has the right soil, light, and space to grow is paramount to long-term vitality. Urban tree stress for established trees can be avoided with proper irrigation, pruning, and the addition of mulch around the base. Research has shown that replacing turf under trees with a few inches of organic mulch significantly improves tree roots by increasing soil aeration and nutrient availability and, most importantly, by removing the grass that is a fierce competitor for the same resources as the tree. Going back to the concept that the tree spent millions of years adapting to a specific environment, the more closely those specific conditions can be recreated for an urban tree, the better chance it has to thrive. A willow is adapted to wetter soils, so its planting site must be kept moist; a pin oak is adapted to acidic soils, so its site must not be too alkaline, and so on. The better the tree's native habitat is understood, the better an arborist can advise on the urban site in which it will perform best.

For trees already suffering and showing symptoms of urban tree stress, action must be taken if the trees are to survive. A tree showing any of the telltale signs indicated here is usually entering advanced stages of decline and will continue in a downward spiral if the source of the stress is not addressed. For this reason, it is extremely important that the cause of the stress and subsequent decline be properly identified before a management plan is implemented. If a tree is treated for boring insects, but the underlying issue was drought, the symptom is temporarily remediated, but a long-term, sustainable solution has not been provided for the tree. The borers will likely return when the insecticide wears off. A full management plan for this tree would be to treat the boring insects to alleviate the immediate stress and then to establish a supplemental irrigation regimen so the tree receives adequate moisture during periods of low rainfall.

Once the source of the stress is identified, a plan can be implemented to address it. Trees in compacted soils can benefit from the use of tools such as the Air-Spade to reduce compaction, incorporate organic matter, and improve aeration. Trees suffering from nutrient deficiencies can be supplemented either through soil application or tree injection, depending on the nutrient necessary. Research has shown that tree growth regulators (TGRs) can improve injured roots on trees by redirecting energy from canopy growth into other structures, including fibrous roots. A TGR should not be seen as a stand-alone treatment for a tree in decline from significant root damage, but when it is combined with other practices, such as air tools, mulching, and proper irrigation, the results can be quite beneficial. Insect and disease pressures are often acute problems that can be addressed using available plant health-care products. Yet, as stated before, if the pest problem is a secondary issue, the primary cause must also be addressed. Of course, not all urban tree stress issues can be helped by an arborist. If a tree is only borderline hardy for an area, it may survive a few mild winters. But no intervention by an arborist can save it from a severe cold snap.

CHAPTER 21
TREE PESTS AND DISEASE

THE THREAT TO THE HEALTH of trees from pests and diseases is something that can't always be avoided. But what is true of humans is also true of trees: a healthy tree is much less likely to succumb to an attack than a tree that is under stress. Sometimes, however, even healthy specimens can fall victim.

Often by the time we notice visible signs of a problem, the effective time to treat has come and gone, so it's prudent to be vigilant and stay ahead of the curve. Sometimes treatments are preventive, especially with regard to certain types of fungi. But most treatments, whether preventive in nature or not, have specific windows of opportunity in which they are effective. The timing is usually contingent upon treating within a particular stage in the development of the pest or disease.

If the best defense is a healthy tree, how do you go about ensuring your trees are at their peak health? It always starts with the basics. Healthy trees must have a suitable soil structure and an adequate supply of nutrients and water. Proper pruning and sufficient room for both the root system and canopy to expand to their full potential are also important. Additionally, healthy trees will not have much damage from cars, lawn mowers, string trimmers, and the like. It's a good idea to have your arborist inspect the trees and make any recommendations that you can follow to improve their health.

The following is a list of the top eleven pest and disease problems that we see in the mid-Atlantic region. It is not an all-inclusive list, but it covers the majority of the culprits that plague the trees in the area.

Hemlock wooly adelgid appears like white powder on hemlock branches.

1. **Hemlock wooly adelgid** originally came to the United States from Asia almost a hundred years ago and spread to the East Coast in the 1950s. Adelgid are tiny insects that suck sap, causing needle drop and dieback (tree demise that proceeds from the most external areas inward) of branches, which often leads to the death of the tree. The telltale sign is a white, woolly substance on the needles and branches. The good news is that hemlock wooly adelgid infestations can be controlled.

2. **Anthracnose** is a twig and leaf fungus found on a number of tree and plant species, especially sycamore, ash, oak, dogwood, and maple. Symptoms can include irregularly shaped markings of different colors that appear on leaves, twigs, flowers, and fruits, sometimes forming cankers on the twigs and branches. Anthracnose may just be unattractive in mild cases, or it may result in the death of the host tree in more severe cases.

3. **Discula anthracnose** is a fungal disease of flowering dogwood trees. It has spread down the Appalachian mountain range from the northeastern states into many of the southern states along the East Coast. The fungi thrive in cool, wet spring weather. It has led

to the decline and death of many flowering dogwoods, especially those growing in shady environments.

4. **Borers** are wood chewers and come in a variety of types, but they generally do their damage by tunneling around under trees' bark. In most cases, borers attack trees that are already under stress. The larvae and adults chew through the vascular system, disrupting the flow of water and nutrients to the canopy of the tree.

5. **Spider mites**, although tiny, can suck the life out of leaves and the soft tissue of your trees. Most spider mites do the majority of their damage in the hot, dry months; however, spruce spider mites are cool-season mites. Populations can increase very quickly, so infestations must be controlled aggressively.

6. **Scale** are small insects that suck the sap out of trees, killing off branches and stems. They overwinter under the bark. There are two main types of scale that attack trees—soft and armored—but there are many species. Scale damage is treatable, if the timing is right.

7. **Eastern tent caterpillars** build unsightly nests and, in large numbers, can defoliate a tree. They tend to infest fruit trees, including apple, cherry, crabapple, hawthorn, maple, plum, pear, and peach trees. Eastern tent caterpillars overwinter as eggs within an egg mass that can contain between 150 and 400 eggs. They hatch around the same time buds open in the spring and start feeding on leaves.

8. **Dutch elm disease** came to the United States from the Netherlands in the 1920s and has had a devastating effect on elm populations. Elm bark beetles spread Dutch elm disease from tree to tree. There are treatments that can control it with a high degree of effectiveness, if applied correctly.

9. **Lace bugs** are tiny insects that feed on the underside of leaves by piercing the leaf to suck out the sap. They attack a wide variety of trees and shrubs and are often not noticed until they have caused significant damage to the host plant.

10. **Bagworm caterpillars** make long, narrow bags that are sometimes mistaken for pinecones. Heavy infestations can defoliate a tree. Several seasons of this may lead to the death of the host tree. Small infestations can be removed by hand; larger infestations can be controlled, but only if the treatment is done with the right timing.
11. **Japanese beetles** attack a wide variety of plants in the eastern United States. They generally start feeding at the top of trees and plants and work their way down in clusters, eating leaves, flowers, and fruit. Most of the damage takes place over a period of about four to six weeks during the warm months, starting in the later part of June.

CHAPTER 22
HEMLOCK WOOLLY ADELGID

The following chapter was written by James Martin, ISA-certified arborist, licensed tree expert, commercial pesticide applicator, and owner of Growing Earth Tree Care in northern Virginia.

Hemlock woolly adelgid

As you might be aware, hemlock woolly adelgid has been a problem for a number of years. The easily identified, telltale sign of woolly adelgid is a white woolly substance that is most obvious on the needles in late spring. (Tree experts get the most service calls at this point, when lower branches start to become visibly affected.) The adelgid feeds on the sap at the base of hemlock needles and chokes off the supply of nutrients. The result is that the needles turn brown and die. Treatments are effective, and it usually doesn't take long to gain control of the pest and reverse the damage.

I have been treating this pest in the urban landscape for quite a while and thought I had a good understanding of the extent of the damage it can cause. However, while I was recently hiking with my family in the Blue Ridge Mountains in southwest Virginia, I saw firsthand the devastating damage that woolly adelgid has done to the native hemlocks. The Cascades is an approximately seventy-foot-tall waterfall located near the top of a mountain in the Jefferson National Forest in Giles County. This particular section of the park is about a half-hour drive from downtown Blacksburg. To view this beautiful natural wonder, you must first hike for approximately two miles, starting at the base of the mountain. The trail winds up the mountain, following Little Stony Creek. Several areas along the way open up to some of the most breathtaking views of the Blue Ridge that Virginia has to offer. It was at one of these vistas that I first noticed how much damage the hemlock woolly adelgid has caused over the past decade. Up close, it was easy to see the unmistakable signs in the foliage of smaller trees. It was unsettling to see large stands of mature, hundred-foot-tall hemlocks, with diameters of over thirty inches, completely dead.

After completing our round-trip hike of over four miles, we ended back at the main area. There were several Federal Forest Service employees available to educate the public about invasive species and their effects on our national forests. (This particular day they were informing the public about garlic mustard, a weed found throughout the Blue Ridge.) I expressed my shock over all the damage I had witnessed on the hemlocks. The foresters were a knowledgeable resource regarding how much damage the pest has done, as well as the different ways in which the forest service was dealing with all the large, dead trees. Removing stands of dead trees on the side of steep mountains can be a daunting task for forest workers. In an effort to avoid damaging the existing trees that would become the future of these mountain ranges, as well as to ensure the safety of the workers on the ground, helicopters were brought in to do the heavy lifting. The helicopters are equipped with a series of cutting blades hanging below the aircraft. They can strip dead trees of all the branches, leaving only the trunk to be felled or possibly left standing for habitat. With help from the helicopters, trees don't have to be felled whole from the ground level. This helps to avoid destroying the surrounding landscape, leaving the smaller trees unscathed for the most part.

The park service has their hands full trying to manage this pest. Biological and chemical treatments have helped subdue the problem. But there are many considerations that the park service has to weigh before deciding on the best plan for implementation when dealing with an area as vast as a national forest. Thankfully, from my perspective, treating harmful pests like the woolly adelgid is a lot easier on smaller properties, such as those in the urban landscape.

CHAPTER 23
BORERS AND THE DAMAGE THEY CAUSE

BORERS ARE THE LARVAE OF beetles or moths. There are over a dozen varieties of borers that attack a multitude of tree species. Unfortunately, these borers can cause tremendous damage and often will kill the host tree. It's important to understand that they are a secondary invader: they attack trees that are already stressed or weakened. Although you can treat to prevent borers or deal with an infestation that is underway, it is imperative to also treat the primary cause of the stress.

Stressed trees emit hormones that attract borers and other pests. Female borers lay their eggs within the crevices of the bark. The larvae hatch and feed by burrowing tunnels into the sapwood or heartwood. This occurs during the peak growing season and disrupts the flow of nutrients and water to the canopy. Water is drawn up from the root system, travels through the trunk's vascular system, and is released through the leaves in a process called transpiration. Transpiration is critical for photosynthesis to take place. When the flow of water is interrupted, photosynthesis does not take place, and the leaves die. The tips of the canopy are farthest from the source of water, so they usually die first.

The good news is that borers can be prevented or treated if caught early enough. An International Society of Arboriculture–certified arborist who is licensed in pesticide application can make recommendations for treatment if the attack has already begun. But complete treatment also requires finding the root cause of the stress that invited the borers in the first place. Often it will be something as simple to correct as an improper amount of water, either too little or too much. Mulching is also an excellent way to improve the health of your trees. The key is to get your tree as healthy as possible.

What are some of the symptoms of a borer attack? Look for small stains along the trunk or around the root flare. Sawdust at the base of the trunk may be a sign that the larvae are drilling into the trunk. Dieback (tree demise that proceeds from the most external areas inward) from some or all of the tops (of the canopy) is another sign. Also look for small, round holes in the trunk. If you see any of these symptoms, call an ISA-certified arborist as soon as possible.

CHAPTER 24
WHY WON'T YOU TOP MY TREES?

Topping destroys the natural beauty of trees and leads to structural problems.

FOR YEARS, HOMEOWNERS HAVE BEEN topping trees in an attempt to control canopy growth and stop roots from causing havoc in their yards. Some people are under the false impression that topping trees makes them safer.

In reality, topping creates structural problems that will weaken a tree over time.

Trees use leaf surface areas to photosynthesize sunlight to produce the food and energy they need. Removal of a large quantity of leaf surface by topping inhibits this process and threatens the tree's overall health, assuming it survives. In a desperate attempt to feed itself, the tree sprouts suckers that grow three times as fast but have only one-third the strength of normal branches.

Flat-topping cuts produce brutal wounds that never properly close, which allows water to pool on the site. It also allows decay and insects to attack the tree from the top down. The central rotting process begins within each growth ring. The situation becomes increasingly more dangerous as new growth above the decayed area gets heavier. High winds and heavy snow often break these weak branches.

Unfortunately, some tree companies still top trees even though, according to the International Society of Arboriculture, "topping results in a potentially hazardous situation and is not a recommended pruning method." Tchukki Andersen, a board-certified master arborist at the Tree Care Industry Association (TCIA) adds, "Millions of trees have been hacked with little or no consideration for their health and structural integrity." According to the TCIA, many topped trees eventually die as a result of the damage. Others eventually become unsafe and suffer dangerous limb breakage. Since there are no arborist licensing requirements in many states—Virginia is one example—it is up to consumers to beware of such faulty practices.

Root growth is not slowed by tree topping; in fact, it can be enhanced. If you are concerned about damage to foundations, sidewalks, driveways, pipes, and so forth, become familiar with proper root training and pruning as real solutions.

If your tree has already been topped, it should be examined by a certified arborist to determine the best course of action. If the tree can be saved, the arborist can take appropriate, remedial measures, such as correcting the topping cuts.

A tree wound triggers a reaction that signals the tree to form boundaries around the wounded area. This is called *compartmentalization of decay in trees* (CODIT), and it is the tree's first line of defense against decay and insect infestation. When topping cuts have been properly corrected, the tree forms a cambium ring that closes around the wounds. This assists the effort of compartmentalization in defending against decay and insect infestation.

Crown restoration can improve the look and structure of a topped tree. Selected sprouts on each main branch stub are chosen to become the permanent branches. These sprouts will eventually form a more natural-looking crown. Restoration will usually take years and may require a series of prunings to be effective.

If the height or spread of a tree has to be decreased, *crown reduction* may help solve the problem. Limbs are cut back to laterals that are at least one-third the size of the parent branch. This will maintain the structural integrity and natural form of the tree. It will also delay the next pruning. Another solution is to apply a plant-growth regulator.

An arborist certified by the International Society of Arboriculture may make these and other recommendations upon completing a visual inspection of the tree. Of course, it's always better to avoid problems in the first place by planting the right tree in the right location.

CHAPTER 25

WHAT MAKES SOME TREES MORE LIKELY TO FAIL DURING A STORM?

It's NOT ALWAYS EASY TO predict which trees will fall victim to a storm, but there are factors that can increase the risk. Take a close look at your trees to see how many of the following risk factors are present.

Limited Root Zone or Damaged Roots

Large trees with limited space for root zones are especially prone to windthrow. Roots that have been structurally compromised from construction, disease, compaction, and other factors fall (no pun intended) into the same category. The root system has several important functions, including anchoring and stabilizing the tree within the soil. Ground saturation from excessive rainfall or irrigation can cause roots to release their grip from the soggy soil and uproot, especially when high winds come into play. Trees with damaged roots will usually fall in the opposite direction of the damage.

Thick, Heavy Canopies

Thick canopies may catch the wind like a sail, which can put tremendous pressure on weak attachment points and the root system, and often leads to structural failure. This is also why live trees seem to create more storm damage than dead trees, although in a storm, any tree can fail. Some species are particularly susceptible to wind damage. They include Bradford pears, maples, and white pines.

Weak Attachment Points

Strong attachment points where the branch meets the trunk are U-shaped. Weak attachment points are V-shaped. As the branch and trunk each grow in diameter, they eventually start to push against each other. Additionally, as the tree grows, bark becomes included within that union, further weakening it. Species susceptible to this defect are Bradford pears, lindens, and maples.

Codominant Leads

Structurally sound trees have one dominant trunk. Trees with two or more dominant leads may suffer storm damage as the trunks blow away and toward each other at varying rates. Furthermore, they frequently have bark included at the union.

Structural Damage

Preexisting structural damage such as vertical cracks, cavities, broken branches, and girdling roots can cause tree failure.

The risk factors mentioned here, individually and collectively, can result in a tree's failure during a storm. However, as the following quote from an article published by the Tree Care Industry Association *testifies, even structurally sound trees can fail if the storm is severe enough*:

> For hardwood trees, such as oak, maple, birch, and ash, a three-second gust of 74 mph will break large (greater than one inch) branches, 91 mph will uproot trees, and 110 mph will snap tree trunks. For softwood trees such as pine, spruce, fir, and hemlock, a three-second gust of 75 mph will break large branches, 87 mph will uproot trees, and 104 mph will snap tree trunks. These are not absolute numbers but a value near the middle of the range of minimum wind speeds expected to cause the damage.
>
> Wind speeds of these magnitudes occur with weak tropical cyclones, weak tornadoes, thunderstorm downbursts, and winds associated with midlatitude cyclones, among other meteorological events. In addition, heavy accumulations of snow or ice may cause trees to fail even with lighter wind speeds.[1]

---

1 Thomas W. Schmidlin, "Deaths from Wind-Related Tree Failures," *Tree Care Industry Association Magazine* (December 2008).

CHAPTER 26

SAFETY AROUND STORM-DAMAGED TREES

Storms can have a devastating effect on trees. If your tree has fallen victim to a recent storm, caution cannot be overemphasized. Hundreds of homeowners are injured or killed each year from storm-damaged trees.

The first cautionary measure to take is to secure the area. Keep bystanders away by using cones, caution tape, signs, and other warning signals as necessary. Curious children are often oblivious to the dangers. Trees leaning on structures or caught up in other trees can shift or continue falling without warning. Never walk beneath or occupy structures below these dangerous trees.

Weekend warriors armed with chainsaws rarely have the experience to deal with risky, storm-damaged trees. These trees are far more hazardous than normal trees due to vertical cracks, multiple high-tension pressure points, rolling or shifting weight, electrocution risk, and other factors that the untrained are not equipped to foresee. These hazards are in addition to the myriad dangers that can come from working with trees, chainsaws, and tremendous weight. The expression, "I know just enough to be dangerous," fits everyone but the professional arborist.

Electrocution is frequently an overlooked peril. Wet trees can and do conduct electricity. Live wires may be hidden from view by a thick canopy. Additionally, fences can carry a charge from down the block when downed wires come into contact with them. Another real danger is the presence of generators that can be switched on at any time and create an electrical backflow through conductors such as fences and downed wires.

Generators are often turned on with no advance warning to the rest of the neighborhood.

Other hazards include broken or hanging branches. They can break loose and fall, endangering people and property alike. The Tree Care Industry Association and other authorities strongly recommend hiring a professional arborist to clean up storm-damaged trees. The level of experience and skill necessary to do this job is far above what the average homeowner possesses. Homeowners commonly use inappropriate equipment, especially ladders, which become the cause of numerous crippling injuries and deaths that could have been avoided. The stump of an uprooted tree can fall back into the hole when the trunk is cut loose from it. Tragically, this has caused the death of small children who were playing in the hole when the tree settled back in.

Even seasoned professionals who work with trees day in, day out are at a high risk of injury or death while cleaning up storm damage. Think twice before attempting to save money by jeopardizing your health and well-being; it's just not worth it.

CHAPTER 27
CABLING SYSTEMS IN TREES

PERHAPS ONE OF THE MAIN causes of the structural failure of trees in an urban environment is a weak attachment point, where two or more codominant trunks meet. Codominant trunks consist of at least two main trunks of similar sizes growing from a single base. In many cases, these junctures are V-shaped. Commonly referred to as V-crotches, or codominant stems, they form an inherently weak connection that often worsens as the tree matures. Each trunk will expand in diameter as the tree grows. Eventually, the trunks start to push against each other, and bark becomes included within the middle of the juncture. The juncture is inherently weak, yet it is necessary to support an ever-increasing weight load.

Predictably, when one of these weak junctures fails, it's usually due to the stress of high winds. In a windstorm, the two trunks tend to sway at different speeds because of their varying weight and canopy size. The speed variation forces them to move toward and away from each other, which puts tremendous force on the already weak junctures. If the force overwhelms the structural integrity of the juncture, the tree will fail.

If you were in the mid-Atlantic region when Hurricane Isabel devastated the area around Washington DC, you might remember the extensive damage it caused. We spent several weeks cleaning up the damage to homes and properties from trees that were not able to survive the high winds. Trees with codominant trunks and V-shaped unions were the cause of the majority of the damage sustained.

But trees with properly installed cabling systems suffered substantially less damage. Certainly, there were branches above some of the cabling systems that were damaged, but generally the damage was minimal when compared with similar trees that had no support system. We saw many cases where entire halves of trees that were not reinforced with a cabling system had failed, often falling onto houses, vehicles, across yards, and into streets. In almost every case we witnessed, trees that had updated cabling systems installed may have sustained damage above the cable, but the installation prevented the entire leader from failing.

Nevertheless, not all types of junctures need to be supported. A union that is U-shaped is a much stronger junction than the weaker, V-shaped one. It generally does not have the problem of one trunk growing into another. Because there is plenty of room for the growth of both leaders, the strength of supporting wood increases with each year's growth. In contrast, in trees with codominant trunks with a V-shaped union, the new supporting wood that comes with each year's growth is inhibited, because the two leaders do not have room to grow individually. However, all too often trees with naturally strong unions will get cabling systems installed that are simply not necessary. Trees that are artificially supported in this way will tend to react accordingly and may actually become dependent on the cabling system.

Of course, an ounce of prevention is worth a pound of cure. The best way to avoid the problems associated with codominant stems and V-shaped unions is with developmental pruning while the tree is young. The developmental pruning of young trees solves several issues when done correctly, one being the removing of codominant trunks. The idea is to create a single dominant trunk that will remain structurally strong as the tree matures. If this is not done when the tree is relatively young, by the time the weak union becomes a structural problem, pruning may no longer be a viable option. Additionally, through developmental pruning, lateral branches along the trunk can be removed in such a way as to leave a good scaffolding branching structure.

If a mature tree has issues with structurally weak junctures, installing a cabling system can help reduce the risk of failure. A properly installed cabling system will allow the two trunks to blow together in unison when heavy winds blow. The two trunks work together to help support each other.

The methods and materials used for cabling trees have come a long way over the past few decades. In the old days, methods included wrapping wire around the trunks, essentially tying the two sides together. The problem with this method is that trees grow in diameter every year, and over time this causes girdling of the trunks. Girdling not only results in severe wounds but also actually chokes the vascular system of the tree. As the tree expands with new growth around the cables, the cable blocks the cambium layer. This is the thin layer of cells from which the xylem and phloem grow—the vascular system that brings water and nutrients up the trunk from the roots to the leaves and carbohydrates and sugars back down the tree.

Newer cabling methods use a material that is flexible. The working theory is that the flexibility of the system allows the tree to move back and forth without permitting the two trunks to separate to the point of failure. This encourages the tree to continue growing the supporting wood that is necessary to handle the forces of windstorms and gravity.

Metal cables are acceptable for use in supporting mature trees. Unlike young trees, they grow slowly and are unlikely to become dependent on the cabling system. Material flexibility is not an issue.

Both systems have their advantages and disadvantages; each has its usefulness in the right situation. Keep in mind that cabling systems can help *reduce* the risk of a catastrophic tree failure, but they cannot eliminate that risk. It's a good idea to have a trained arborist inspect cables periodically to see if they need adjusting or updating.

CHAPTER 28

WILL YOUR CONSTRUCTION PROJECT KILL YOUR TREES?

Do you have plans for a new construction project? If so, it makes a lot of sense to take into consideration the impact it may have on your trees before you get started. The following factors explain why construction almost always has a negative effect on the health of nearby trees:

- Root damage
- Changes in grade and water flow
- Chemicals introduced into the soil
- Variations in sunlight and wind flow

Unfortunately, the thought of tree preservation on construction sites often takes place after the damage has become evident in the trees. At that point, it is at best a game of catch-up and at worst a race against time to try to mitigate the extent of the destruction. Construction projects don't have to be large additions or brand-new buildings to cause significant damage to the surrounding trees. The projects can be as simple as replacing underground pipe or wires to the house.

Larger projects, such as additions to existing structures and new construction, often require a tree-preservation plan to be included with the submitted plans. These plans will usually require a certified arborist to help put them together based upon some of the criteria listed below. When a large portion of the existing tree canopy is to be removed during the construction process, the planting of new trees is often a requirement. It is advantageous from both an aesthetic and a monetary point of view to preserve existing trees in many cases. Mature trees are far more valuable than newly planted saplings.

The best time to call your arborist is at the planning stage, before anything has been set in stone. He will want to conduct an inventory of the affected trees that will take into consideration their size and value as a species, their current health, and the likelihood that they will survive the construction process, among other things. If a tree is unlikely to remain vibrant and healthy, it is wiser to remove it before placing a structure underneath it, as this often saves a lot of money in the long run. It takes a lot more time, and therefore money, to remove a tree while having to carefully work around a structure beneath it. At this stage in the process, you may find it advantageous to adjust the location of the structure's footprint in order to preserve the root system of a valuable specimen tree rather than risk losing the tree altogether.

The arborist will be particularly interested in preserving as much of the root zone as possible. The more the root system is left intact, the less impact the construction will have on the tree. This will often involve negotiation between the arborist and the contractor. It is important for both sides to be realistic as to the needs of the other. Once a tree protection line is set, it is important that the line not be breached during construction. There are some construction techniques that can help preserve roots, such as the use of footings for walls. The Air-Spade is a tool that can be used to find roots before they get damaged.

Root zones are protected by the installation of temporary fencing that establishes tree-preservation areas. The fencing is usually made of four-foot-high welded wire with clearly marked signs about every thirty feet. The signs should say something like "Keep Out, Tree-Preservation Area" in both English and Spanish. Absolutely no construction materials or equipment are to be placed over the root zone. Another thing to be proactive about is the disposal of materials like paint, paint thinner, and other products that are harmful or toxic to roots. It is helpful to put in place fines for any violations or encroachments that take place during the construction phase. This can be put into the contract prior to acceptance and goes a long way toward ensuring compliance.

Silt fencing is often installed at the limits of a clearing to keep silt and other runoff from accumulating over root zones. This is often a requirement of local officials for approval of the site plans.

An arborist may recommend that roots be pruned just outside the tree-preservation line. This avoids getting the roots torn by construction equipment, which can cause considerable damage well within the protected root zone. Pruning of roots leaves clean cuts that are far better for the tree. The arborist may also recommend that a thick layer of wood-chip mulch be temporarily placed over roots that may otherwise become compacted by heavy equipment. He or she may also recommend deep-root fertilizing to replenish nutrients.

New construction may change the manner in which water flows across the property. It can make formerly dry areas wet and vice versa. The change in water flow can adversely affect tree health, and steps should be taken to avoid this possibility.

A variety of chemicals can be introduced to the soil during construction. These may come from careless workers cleaning paintbrushes outside or even originate in the runoff of chemicals within construction materials. New cement may change the nearby soil pH. Containment of these inevitable chemical pollutants within the construction zone is important. Proper handling and cleanup of equipment and construction material guidelines should be agreed upon prior to contracts being signed.

Construction does not have to lead to the death of your trees. With a little planning and foresight, your trees can live a long and healthy life. Don't wait until after the damage is done before you call your arborist. If you have already completed a construction project, it's prudent to have an arborist take a look at your trees and make recommendations to mitigate any damage that may already have taken place.

CHAPTER 29

HOMEOWNER ASSOCIATIONS AND THEIR TREES

The following chapter was written by Linda Paine, former tree committee chair of the Deepwood Homeowner Association in Reston, Virginia.

IF A TREE FALLS IN the woods, does it matter? That depends. It does if it falls near or on houses, parking lots, or walkways. Homeowner associations (HOAs) with common-area trees have an important responsibility for the well-being and safety of their residents.

As a long-term resident of our community association, I have served for many years on the "tree committee," although it was often a committee of one. The purpose of this article is to pass along to you some of my experiences in caring for our association's trees.

Well-cared-for trees are valuable and important assets. They certainly improve the overall quality of life and enjoyment of the residents. Homeowner associations often have trees that were planted by the developer and residents. Additionally, a community may have natural woodland areas. However they got there, trees come with the need for responsible stewardship—whether Mother Nature planted the trees or not.

Tree care, which sometimes includes the removal of trees, is important for the safety of residents and their properties. Trees are stronger and healthier when deadwood and weakly attached branches are removed. Thinning of the crown allows greater air movement and light penetration. Storms and strong winds can be very destructive to trees with heavy leaf cover and thick crowns. Severe weather can cause a healthy tree with a fully leafed-out crown to uproot and fall over. Weak or dead branches can be lethal when falling to the ground. When tree care is not administered on a continuing basis, small problems can become larger. As with people, early detection and treatment is often much more cost effective than ignoring the issue until it's become a much bigger problem.

Communities often discover that tree plantings done years prior now include problem trees. For example, the Bradford pear has been heavily planted in many communities nationwide. Over the years, however, the structural problems associated with that tree have become a huge liability for a large number of those communities. In communities that relied heavily on the Bradford pear, storms have damaged the trees so badly that a large asset has been lost. Hence another concern for homeowner associations: be careful not to overplant any particular species.

The budget for tree care should always be well funded. Liability is a big issue when we live in communities with trees. We live in a litigious society and have insurance to cover our houses, cars, health, and other financial burdens. A proactive tree-care program can reduce insurance claims against your association. You are also less likely to be considered liable when damage occurs if you can demonstrate that you have been proactive. If you have a well-documented tree-maintenance history, insurance companies and courts are more likely to consider these occurrences "acts of God," for which you are not liable. A long-term tree-care program with a proactive focus helps keep your trees in the best condition possible and saves you money in the long run.

So, what are some of the things to look for if you live in a community with common-ground trees? Below is a sample list of some tree issues commonly experienced in a residential community.

1. Limbs or branches of a tree should not be touching your house or causing difficulty for those entering or exiting properties.

Branches rubbing against structures can result in damage to both the tree and the structure.
2. Tree branches should not scrape the tops of cars. Proper clearance over streets and parking should be maintained. Keep in mind that moisture after a rain can make branches sag down more than when they're dry.
3. Sidewalks should be clear of any branches that might cause injury to the residents.
4. Broken and dangling limbs can cause injury if they fall on a resident or private property.
5. A large amount of deadwood may signal a serious problem with the health of that tree.
6. Trees with leans should be inspected by an arborist on a regular basis.
7. Dead trees should be brought down to a safe height or removed entirely if they pose a risk to nearby structures.

The structural problems of this tree and its proximity to the street make it a high priority for removal.

Tree care should always include a qualified arborist. The International Society of Arboriculture and the Tree Care Industry Association are good sources when considering the need for a tree-care program in your community. Your county can also give guidance in finding a good tree service. I strongly recommend against using an unqualified and poorly trained tree service, because it will not be in the best interest of your community. You may actually put your residents at greater risk for injury and liability by employing the wrong tree company in an effort to save a little money.

If your HOA has a managing agent or tree/landscape committee, homeowners should report any concerns to them. Careful records should be kept of the concerns or requests for tree work. If an arborist is walking the community, he or she should have those concerns on a list so they can be evaluated.

Some communities are quite large and may benefit from more than one resident monitoring the trees. It might be helpful to divide the community into areas and then ask committee members to look at the trees in their area on a regular basis, especially after heavy weather events. Homeowners do not always notice when a tree has been damaged and often don't report it to the managing agent if they do see a problem. However, a committee member responsible for a particular area can assess those trees and report any damage. A checklist of what to look for might be helpful.

Homeowners should not attempt to work on any common-ground tree. Not only is there a risk the work will be done poorly, but the liability issue is significant. Homeowners should be well versed in what can or cannot be done on the common areas. In cases where there are limited funds to do the tree work, the HOA might agree to let the homeowner pay for the service as long as it is performed by an approved tree company.

Healthy trees are wonderful assets for your community. When properly cared for, they add tremendous beauty and value, including cleaner and cooler air, and they benefit local wildlife. Their benefits to your lifestyle, too, are well worth the effort.

CHAPTER 30

IS YOUR TREE STRUCTURALLY SOUND?

The following chapters were authored by Lew Bloch. Lew Bloch is a nationally known ASCA registered consulting arborist/landscape architect with over forty years of experience. He is the author of Tree Law Cases in the USA, Bloch Publishing Co Inc (2000) *and coauthor of* The Guide for Plant Appraisal *(9th edition, International Society of Arboriculture, 2000), has been a contributor for many publications, and has lectured in several capacities. He has testified in numerous law cases involving fatalities, personal injuries, property damage, neighbor disputes, negligence cases, appraisals of monetary values, and other situations. He frequently performs tree risk assessments for homeowners, insurance companies, and municipalities.*

IN ANALYZING A TREE'S CONDITION, health and structural stability are both important; but with regard to safety issues, structural stability is more important. The questions are basically the same because they are brought up by tree owners and tree managers in regard to the second question about safety. Sometimes my clients raise their eyebrows when I tell them that in a severe weather event such as Hurricane Sandy or a derecho, quite often the healthy trees topple over, and the sick ones remain upright.

When trees topple (completely uproot) in these types of events, it is usually from a combination of high winds and saturated soil. The reason that the trees with large, dense, healthy canopies fall over is known as the *sail effect*. The effect of the winds against these branches is similar to wind affecting the sail on a sailboat. When the soil is saturated at the same time, the anchoring roots can no longer perform their function of holding the tree upright. A sick tree is usually sparse, and the sail effect is no longer a problem. If the sick tree has a lot of dead and dying branches, these could break and fall during the storm—but the tree is not likely to uproot. Likewise, if a tree has an advanced root decay problem, it could topple.

In some instances, this failure, where the entire tree falls over, may actually be considered a soil failure rather than a tree failure. Of course, if the tree falls on your house, it may not make any difference to you.

Tree health is usually considered to be an insect or disease problem, but in reality, most of our tree inspection situations as arborists (consulting as well as contracting arborists) are *abiotic* in nature. This means they are not related to insect or disease problems. Following are some of the most common types of abiotic problems we encounter.

- Strangulating/girdling roots (Tree roots should radiate away from the tree trunk, not circle around it. This is a very common problem.)
- Trees planted too deeply (This is much more common than it should be.)
- Too much mulch and/or soil against the tree trunk or trunk flare (This is another very common situation.)
- Nearby construction damage
- Change of grade on the root zone
- Compacted soil on the root zone
- Poor branch and/or trunk structure (This is very common because of multistem trees.)
- Severe tree lean
- Improper pruning practices, such as leaving tree stubs or tree topping
- Leaving twine or wire baskets on trees when planting them
- Cracks/seams in the tree trunk
- Large street tree in a small planting area between the sidewalk and curb

There are also occurrences of trees affected by more than one of the described situations.

Tree inspections by a certified arborist on a regular basis are desirable and quite important to a tree owner or tree manager. Some contracting arborists may do this free for their regular customers, but consulting arborists charge a fee for this service. It has nothing to do with ethics or honesty, but tree contractors are in business to sell tree services, and consulting arborists are only selling advice and opinions. Some arboricultural documents recommend trees be inspected on an annual basis.

There are different types of tree inspections. The most basic is what is called a drive-by or windshield inspection, which is done while driving along the road, looking for possible danger signs that may affect the roadway. Of course, this is the methodology used by municipalities and highway administrations for situations where there are numerous trees. This method is used because of cost factors and may miss many possible defects. For most homeowners and small properties, the arborist does a complete walk around the entire tree, usually with hand tools and binoculars, looking down (to where the root system is) as well as looking up into the canopy. If called for, further diagnoses may be needed. These could include soil or tissue-sample analysis by a laboratory, decay inspection with a resistograph-type tool (a drill that prints out a reading of wood quality as it goes into the tree, similar to an EKG reading), testing with a TreeRadar inspection (a ground-penetrating system that can show decay in tree trunks as well as underground roots), a root collar excavation, or possibly climbing into the tree's canopy.

There is a relatively new national program for tree risk-assessment certification for arborists. After classroom and field exercises, the arborist takes a written exam. After passing this test, a certificate is issued. This entire process needs to be repeated every four years.

Without going into detail, the tree risk-assessment process involves point systems and a chart to arrive at "tree failure" potential for the entire tree—or perhaps for a given tree part. Although the tree risk literature discusses problems during severe weather events (wind, rain, snow, ice), the rating system does not actually reflect these possibilities. Often a tree that has decay or structural flaws that would not be a high risk during normal weather events could be dangerous during a severe weather event. This potential needs to be considered for trees that are close to houses or other high-value targets.

The final decisions of tree risk management lie with the property owner or property manager, not with the arborist. The arborist's role is that of an advisor rather than of a decision maker. Tree owners and managers may have different levels of risk tolerance.

Again, there is no such thing as a safe tree. Trees can be made "safer," but they cannot be made "safe." Furthermore, trees can be managed, but they cannot be controlled, and to live near a tree is to accept some degree of risk. The only way to eliminate all tree risks is to remove all trees.

CHAPTER 31

CONSULTING ARBORISTS

SO WHAT EXACTLY IS A consulting arborist? The third edition of the book *Arboriculture* by Richard Harris, James Clark, and Nelda Matheny defines the term as someone who "[will] provide technical expertise including problem diagnosis, management problems, and tree appraisals *rather than* perform service work" (emphasis added).

In fact, however, many consulting arborists do both consulting and contracting. There is nothing wrong with a tree contractor performing consultations for a fee, free of charge, or as a deposit applied to future tree services. Consulting is a common procedure in many businesses and can be a good sales tool. But such persons may not be independent consultants providing unbiased opinions if they are doing both, as there may be some financial gain to be made from the consultation. In order to arrive at an independent opinion or report, the consultant should not be permitted to bid on performing the tree-contracting services. This situation could result in the consultant inspecting and supervising his or her own specifications. This may or may not be a conflict of interest, but it could appear to be a perceived conflict.

You must assume that any consultation could wind up as a lawsuit. If someone provides a report regarding the appraisal of monetary tree values or the condition or health of a tree and also provides a bid on providing services to the tree, his or her credibility of expressing an unbiased opinion is gone. I have seen this done several times. For example, there was a case in which the plaintiff sued three separate parties for the value of a forty-six-inch-diameter oak tree the plaintiff claimed was killed due to the construction of a new home. I found a photo in a large group of photos taken the day construction started and provided by the plaintiff in discovery. Other trees in the background were in full leaf, and this tree was extremely weak with very little foliage—actually dying at that time. Several tree companies provided reports about the tree's condition (some mentioned *Armillaria* root-rot disease) and estimates to "save" the tree, and some did appraisals of the monetary value. There were many conflicts of interest here.

It seems as if there are always new situations that occur in consulting; some are unique and interesting, and some are amusing. The following are some of the usual services that consulting arborists perform:

Plant diagnosis. "What is wrong with my tree? Can you save it? Will my dead tree come back?" (Yes, we do hear this, but dead is dead, and dead does *not* come back.) While most clients want to know if their tree is healthy, it is probably more important for safety purposes to ask if the tree is structurally sound. A tree can be healthy but have other problems that make it a high-risk tree. Most of the time in my tree inspections, I find the problem is *abiotic*, not insect or disease related. Furthermore, I find that the most common problem is too much mulch or soil along with the fact that the tree was planted too deep. Sometimes all of the above are exacerbated by irrigation systems. (I have had numerous situations where irrigation systems have severely damaged or killed trees and shrubs.) Some of these problems typically don't have an impact on the trees until some ten to twenty years later. A few years ago, I was retained by a homeowner of a large estate in Montgomery County, Maryland, who could not find out why her trees were doing so poorly. She had seven ISA-certified arborists before me inspect her trees. Some made comments about drought, some wanted to fertilize or spray, and some just did not know. The problem was that for over twelve years, the landscapers kept piling mulch on top of mulch to a height of around twenty-four inches on the tree trunks. Even the sickly azaleas and other bushes had twelve inches of mulch against their stems.

Tree risk assessments. "Is my tree safe?" Of course, there is no such thing as a safe tree; while trees can be made "safer," they cannot be made safe. Also, although we can judge tree risks and make predictions for normal weather conditions, all bets are off during severe weather. In fact, during certain weather conditions of strong winds and saturated soil, the healthy trees will topple, and the sickly trees will remain standing. As I described in the previous chapter, this is caused by the sail effect—a tree with lots of healthy leaves catching more wind than the sparse, dying tree. Actually, this type of failure might be a soil failure, not a tree failure. The amount of risk that is acceptable for a tree is totally up to the tree owner/manager, not the arborist who is the tree advisor.

Opinions to lawyers and insurance companies on legal matters. There are a wide variety of legal matters involving trees such as fatalities, personal injuries, property damage, and property-line issues. These can become contentious and emotional and often are based on negligence or lack of diligence. Some even wind up in criminal court.

Appraisal of the monetary value of plants and landscaping. Sometimes these appraisals are necessary because of the legal and insurance claims already mentioned, but often they are proactive situations rather than damage claims. Some of these are to appraise the value of trees in case they do become damaged, some are for estate purposes, and some are to justify budgets for municipalities. Unfortunately, most appraisal issues involve damage or destruction of plants, sometimes accidental and sometimes intentional.

Preparation, evaluation, and supervision of tree and landscape contracts, plans, and specifications. A consulting arborist frequently becomes involved in these situations, preferably in the early planning stages rather than at the last minute or after problems are noticed.

There are numerous times when tree-service contractors have clients who raise the point that a competitor disagreed with their opinion, such as whether a tree can be treated or needs to be removed, or who may want a second opinion. The contractor may suggest that the client retain a consulting arborist for an independent opinion, because we are selling advice, not contracting services, and do not have a vested financial interest in the opinions.

If someone wishes to retain the services of a consulting arborist or wants to know more about the concept, they should contact the American Society of Consulting Arborists (ASCA) at 301-947-0483 or visit **www.asca-consultants.org**. The highest designation of consulting arboriculture is that of a registered consulting arborist.

A consulting arborist takes the position of being an advocate for the truth—or put another way, an advocate for the tree—not necessarily an advocate for the client. We never know when a seemingly simple project can evolve into a legal matter and end up in court. As a consultant and possible expert witness, we must be comfortable with our opinions and conclusions or we will look like fools on the witness stand. Actually, more than 90 percent of lawsuits never go to court; they settle. But we are never certain which ones will and which ones won't actually see the courtroom.

As I stated, we become involved in many different, sometimes strange situations. We need to know a great deal about many things, but we also need to recognize that, if presented with a situation outside of our expertise, we need to turn down the assignment or retain an expert in that specific field as part of a team project.

As consulting arborists, we have the same or similar backgrounds, training, and expertise in tree, landscape, and nursery industries as tree contractor companies. We are selling our knowledge and opinions rather than actual contracting services.

CHAPTER 32
PROPERTY-LINE DISPUTES

Please remember that this chapter was not written by an attorney. One must seek legal advice from an attorney to interpret any of the aspects of the following or any advice for personal situations.

The neighbor on the right permanently damaged this jointly owned tree by removing every branch growing over his property.

As a full-time consulting arborist and landscape architect, one of the most common situations that I face involves boundary-line trees and borderline trees. A boundary-line tree is one in which the property line goes through any portion of the tree trunk. It could be 2 percent on one side and 98 percent on the other side, but both parties own the tree equally and need to have the other party's permission to do anything to the tree. A borderline tree is located near the property line but has roots and/or branches that extend over the property line. This tree is owned by the party where the tree trunk is located. There have been instances when a borderline tree trunk grows large enough to cross the property line, and it becomes a jointly owned boundary-line tree.

In this chapter, I will address general property issues involving trees. Some of these disputes involve insurance companies, some involve lawyers, and many of them are individual homeowners' disputes that can and do become quite emotional. Even though probably less than 5 percent of all lawsuits go to actual trial, I have testified in two cases that made it to criminal court.

Some of these homeowners' disputes involve major damage to trees as depicted in the photo above from an actual case with which I was involved. The two neighbors in this case took self-help measures to deal with a tree growing over their properties, and each trespassed as a result. In some states, such as Maryland, an injured party may collect treble damages (three times the appraised value of damages) in trespassing situations, and some states allow double damages. Of course, these situations need a consultant to arrive at the monetary value of damages, which could be more than the mere value of the trees and plants. The total amount of damages could include many things such as cleanup, plant establishment costs, maintenance, or legal and consultation fees.

Some disputes involve only minor damages, such as cutting limbs off a 150-year-old oak tree or cutting down trees in a woodland situation. In the oak tree scenario, the tree may not have been damaged at all, perhaps even helped. In the woodland tree situation, the value of the cut trees may only be the firewood value of the tree parts. Even though an illegal trespass may have occurred in these cases, we must explain to the client, who may be very upset, that the monetary value of damages in the claim may not be worth the effort. Again, these are quite emotional experiences for the homeowner. On the other hand, I have been involved in appraisal cases in excess of one million dollars. Interestingly enough, after listening to prospective clients on the telephone describing these situations, I often ask if they are having any other problems with the neighbor besides the tree. The response is often, "Yes, how did you know?"

If a person is having problems with a neighbor's tree encroaching on his or her property, there may be self-help remedies, depending on the state. However, there is a difference between a tree being a nuisance (branches, trunk, or roots causing damage) and a tree being an inconvenience (a tree dropping leaves, twigs, or fruit).

A very old concept of self-help remedies with regard to neighboring trees is called the *Massachusetts Rule*. It stated that a party could cut back any portion of the neighbor's tree, including branches, roots, and tree trunk, as long as the person did not cross the property line. This concept has been gradually superseded because the extent of cutting could, and did, either kill the tree or make it unsafe.

In some states, the Massachusetts Rule has gradually been replaced with what is known as the *Hawaii Rule*. This gives leeway for homeowners to force their neighbor to abate a nuisance (but not merely an inconvenience) if it is doing harm or posing an imminent threat.

Recently, the Supreme Court of Virginia handed down a decision that recognized the Hawaii Rule, and some are now calling this the *Virginia Rule*.

CHAPTER 33

HOW MUCH IS THAT TREE WORTH?

THE APPRAISAL OF THE MONETARY value of plants and landscaping ranges from pretty simple to complex. It is my opinion that numerous plant appraisers make it more complicated than necessary.

Following is a general discussion of the plant appraisal industry. There may be a difference between the cost of plants and the value of plants. In other words, the cost to furnish and install a plant *might* be different from the actual monetary value of that plant. Although trees are part of the real estate, they can have a separate value from the real estate. As strange as it may sound, it is possible for a tree (or trees) to have a value greater than the total property value.

The process of placing monetary value on plants was first used over one hundred years ago, and that process has morphed into today's procedure. Originally, the basic tree cost used in establishing these values was the same throughout the country, but this changed with the realization that prices and costs varied geographically. Other processes and techniques have also changed and improved.

Originally published in 1957, *The Guide for Plant Appraisal* is the bible of plant and landscape appraising. Currently in its ninth edition, the book continues to be tweaked and expanded, and the tenth edition is being developed at the time of this writing. It is authored by the Council of Tree and Landscape Appraisers, which is composed of delegates from the seven green-industry associations. These are the American Nursery and Landscape Association, American Society of Consulting Arborists,

American Society of Landscape Architects, Professional Landcare Network, Association of Consulting Foresters of America, International Society of Arboriculture, and the Tree Care Industry of America. I served on the council from 1994 to 2007, and I coauthored the ninth edition.

Many people may think the only reason to know the value of trees and landscaping is for establishing values for plants that have been destroyed or damaged. But there are many other reasons for needing these values, such as possible property-damage losses for the IRS (quite complex now), estate value purposes, educational or budget purposes, zoning requirements, maintenance needs, and to establish values in case of future damage. There have been developers who have had their large trees appraised and then hung signs with the dollar value on each of the trees in the event the trees were damaged during construction.

There are three basic approaches to establishing values:

- **The cost approach** is the most common approach used for tree and landscape situations. A basic cost is established, which is often depreciated.
- **The income approach** is used when the landscape entities actually produce some type of income. The entities include orchards, nurseries, Christmas tree farms, and even properties where specific trees are important and consumers pay fees for admittance.
- **The market approach** is used in situations similar to real estate appraisals in which comparison costs (comps) are available.

As stated, the cost approach is one used for most landscape appraisals. There are different methods within this approach that are used for these assignments, as follows:

- **The Replacement-Cost Method** is commonly used for plants that are of a size that can be reasonably purchased from a nursery. The basic cost of the plant is depreciated three times. It is depreciated once for the tree species (a Japanese red maple is more valuable than a wild mulberry tree); once for the tree condition (a healthy tree with good structure is more valuable than a sick tree or one with structural flaws); and once for the tree location, which includes the actual site (a tree growing on a well-maintained and well-landscaped site in front of a picture window is more valuable than one on a poorly maintained property or in a woodland setting).

A very large tree being transplanted

* **The Trunk-Formula Method** is commonly used for a tree that is too large to be commonly transplanted from a nursery. It is also a depreciated-cost method in which the basic tree cost, determined regionally, is depreciated three times, as described earlier. With the advent of extra-large tree transplanting methods, these large trees can be appraised by either of these two methods. The photo here shows a very large tree actually being transplanted in a landscape. Therefore, the cost of the tree and its installation is a real cost that can be supported.

- **The Cost-of-Cure Method** is used in instances in which the damages cannot be replicated, but the property can be restored to approximate its precasualty condition. This can be for a single tree that cannot be replicated because of its size or its unusual species, or it can be for a woodland area that has been damaged or destroyed. An additional submethod that is sometimes used is called the Compounded-Interest Method or Years-to-Parity Method. A time period is estimated for the substitute tree(s) to reach parity, and an interest rate is applied for this amount of time to arrive at a value. Using the Cost-of-Cure Method to determine the costs of maintaining the regenerating trees, as well as compounded interest until parity is reached, is appropriate here.
- **The Cost-of-Repair Method** is used when trees have been damaged but not destroyed, and they can be expected to resume normal growth within a reasonable time.

The species factor is determined regionally across the country because the amenity value of trees varies greatly in different climates, both functionally and aesthetically. It even varies within geographic regions. The condition and location factors are determined by the individual plant appraiser's expertise and experience in examining the site or documentation of trees that sometimes are no longer available. Is this subjective? If the appraiser has the appropriate background and experience in the industry, it is my opinion that the process is "subjectively objective." The basic tree cost used in the Trunk-Formula Method is also determined regionally, because costs do vary within the country. In most regions, all of the data is published and periodically reviewed. In some situations, the plant appraiser may decide to use a 100 percent rating for any or all of the depreciating factors.

There are times when the plant appraiser is asked to appraise the monetary value of damaged plants that are in a woodland setting, possibly illegally logged for timber. Of course, this is a trespass even if the encroachment may have been accidental. Many times this requires a forester using an income approach rather than an arborist or landscaper using cost methods, because the trees were not likely amenity trees. But there may be times when the woodlands may be a landscape feature, and the Cost-of-Cure Method would be used for restoration of the woodlands. In some states, such as Maryland, treble damages (three times the appraised value) may be awarded in trespass cases.

Also, there may be times when a large tree being appraised may have no value, or even a negative value, because it is so unhealthy or structurally unsound that it is going to fail in the near future. This tree is no longer an asset; it is a liability. The value *may* be a negative number, as the cost of removal could be used as the negative number.

The Guide for Plant Appraisal is called a "guide" intentionally because it is intended to assist plant appraisers in making decisions to arrive at *an opinion of value*. It does *not* represent the rules or regulations of plant appraising; therefore, experienced appraisers must make their own decisions. Each situation has its own characteristics, and it depends on the assignment provided to the appraiser. In some cases, these decisions need to be based on regional laws and regulations, in which case the appraiser needs to attain guidance from an attorney.

As I stated in the beginning, some appraisals are simple, and some are quite complex. Also, some are quite emotional, and some are even amusing.

ABOUT THE AUTHOR

PAUL FRANCIS MARTIN IS AN ISA-certified arborist and co-owner of Growing Earth Tree Care, located in northern Virginia. He cowrote the "Tree Doc" column for the *Journal Newspapers*. He is a member of the executive board of directors of the mid-Atlantic chapter of the International Society of Arboriculture and is a past president of that organization. Paul has been an arborist since 1988 and lives with his family in Ashburn, Virginia.

Made in the USA
Charleston, SC
06 March 2015